Left Behind

Left Behind

Why voters deserted social democracy –
and how to win them back

John Mills

CIVITAS

First Published
October 2019

© Civitas 2019
55 Tufton Street
London SW1P 3QL

email: books@civitas.org.uk

ISBN 978-1-912581-00-9

Independence: Civitas: Institute for the Study of Civil Society is
a registered educational charity (No. 1085494) and a company
limited by guarantee (No. 04023541). Civitas is financed from
a variety of private sources to avoid over-reliance on any
single or small group of donors.
All the Institute's publications seek to further its objective of
promoting the advancement of learning. The views expressed
are those of the authors, not of the Institute.

Typeset by Typetechnique

Printed in Great Britain
by 4edge Limited, Essex

Contents

Author   vii

Foreword   ix

Introduction: The demise of social democracy   1

1. The embrace of neoliberalism and the decline of economic growth   9

2. The UK's unbalanced economy   29

3. The left-behind and the limits of redistribution   45

4. Coming apart: the cleavages opening up within society   63

5. Moving on from neoliberalism, where next for the centre-left?   81

Conclusion: It's the economy, stupid   98

Notes   103

Author

John Mills is an entrepreneur and economist with a life-long political background in the Labour Party, leading him to becoming its largest individual donor. He graduated in Philosophy, Politics and Economics from Merton College, Oxford, in 1961. He is currently Chairman of John Mills Limited (JML), a consumer goods company specialising in selling products requiring audio-visual promotion at the point of sale, based in the UK but with sales throughout the world. He was Member of Camden Council, specialising in Housing and Finance, almost continuously from 1971 to 2006, with a break during the late 1980s when he was Deputy Chairman of the London Docklands Development Corporation. He was a Parliamentary candidate twice in 1974 and for the European Parliament in 1979.

John has been Secretary of the Labour Euro-Safeguards Campaign since 1975 and the Labour Economic Policy Group since 1985. He has also been a committee member of the Economic Research Council since 1997 and is now its Vice-Chairman. During the period running up to the June 2016 referendum he was Chair of The People's Pledge, Co-Chairman of Business for Britain, Chair of Labour for a Referendum, Chair and then Vice Chair of Vote Leave and Chair of Labour Leave, which became independent of Vote Leave two months before the referendum.

John is the author of numerous pamphlets and articles and he is a frequent commentator on radio and television. He is Chair of The Pound Campaign which regularly produces bulletins advocating that economic policy should be far more focused on the exchange rate than it has been for many decades, arguing that an over-valued pound has been largely responsible for UK deindustrialisation and our seriously unbalanced economy. He is the author or joint-author of twelve books, these being: *Growth and Welfare: A New*

Policy for Britain (Martin Robertson and Barnes and Noble, 1972); *Monetarism or Prosperity* (with Bryan Gould and Shaun Stewart; Macmillan 1982); *Tackling Britain's False Economy* (Macmillan 1997); *Europe's Economic Dilemma* (Macmillan 1998); *America's Soluble Problems* (Macmillan 1999); *Managing the World Economy* (Palgrave Macmillan 2000); *A Critical History of Economics* (Palgrave Macmillan 2002 and Beijing Commercial Press 2006); *Exchange Rate Alignments* (Palgrave Macmillan, 2012), *Call to Action* (with Bryan Gould, Ebury Publishing 2015); *The Real Sterling Crisis* (with Roger Bootle, Civitas 2016) *Britain's Achilles Heel – Our Uncompetitive Pound* (Civitas 2017) and *Economic Growth Post Brexit* (Bite-Sized Books 2019).

Foreword

We live in strange times, as old certainties fade away. I have been a Labour Party supporter all my adult life – and I still am. The party I joined nearly 60 years ago, however, is not the same as the one which exists now. Indeed, the whole political environment has obviously altered dramatically. Like many other people, I am trying to feel my way through all these changes.

My affiliation to the Labour Party does not stem from enthusiasm for all its detailed policies, for I have always been sceptical about some of them. It comes from a general belief that rich people are in a better position to look after themselves than others who are not so fortunate. If we are going to have a society which is reasonably at ease with itself, I think that policies ought to be broadly about making sure that some constraints both politically and economically are put on the wealthy and well connected, to provide room for giving a leg up to people who are not so privileged.

My natural political home, therefore, has always been in the moderate left, social democratic part of the political spectrum. Evidently, however, judging by what has been happening both in the UK and elsewhere in the West, this space is under severe threat of either being abandoned or of being taken over by people and parties with other aspirations and values. Some left-of-centre parties, such as the UK Labour Party, have moved to the left, vacating much of the space it used to occupy. Others, on the continent of Europe, have stayed in roughly the same place but have seen their electoral support decline drastically. PASOK in Greece and the Parti Socialiste in France have more or less imploded.

These developments have taken place at a time when other parts of the political spectrum have seen new political parties, which have often gained large-scale traction only recently, becoming much more significant. The Brexit Party in the UK, Podemos in Spain, the AfD in Germany, the National Rally in France, and the Lega and Five Star movements in Italy, are clearly here to stay. Reacting to these new movements has not only caused the traditional left major problems; it has also put centre right-of-centre parties under severe strain. Politics no longer seem to operate on the left/right axis with which everyone was familiar but now on a new spectrum where attitudes, values and empathy are much more important determinants of the way people vote.

Why has all this happened? This book sets out to try to find some answers to this question and then to use them as a basis for suggesting what might be done to get social democracy back on track again. It seems to me that there are clear reasons why centre left politics have gone into eclipse and that there are steps which could be taken to enable the core values of social democracy – care for the less fortunate combined with opportunities for everyone, achieved through rationality, tolerance and a willingness to compromise – to flourish again. I think there ought to be a political home which is not in eclipse for people who share these goals.

Introduction

The demise of social democracy

This book is about potentially existential threats to moderate left-of-centre political parties across the western world – including the UK. It argues that, with their current key policies, programmes and attitudes, most of them, having lost power, may struggle to regain it again in the foreseeable future. The danger then is that their electoral support dwindles to a point where secular decline sets in, rather as happened to the Liberal Party in the UK during the first quarter of the twentieth century, as they cease to be worthwhile political career vehicles for able people with moderate left-of-centre inclinations. Membership declines and with it the capacity to fight elections and to maintain a major role in local government, let alone national parliaments. In the UK, moderate Labour MPs have had a significant foretaste of this condition since Jeremy Corbyn gained the leadership of the Labour Party. Much more of the dispiriting powerlessness they are experiencing at present may lie in store for them, unless radical changes are made.

On definitions, the text which follows refers to the moderate left of centre as being social democratic rather than democratic socialist. There is a lot of confusing nomenclature about, but everyone involved in politics knows the difference between the moderate and the harder left – and the moderate and harder right too. This book is about why electoral support has ebbed away from the particular part of the political spectrum occupied by social democracy – the centre left – while other segments of the political axis seem to be gaining at social democracy's expense. It then goes on to discuss what might be done to stop this happening.

Something has certainly gone very far awry with social democracy in recent years, not only in the UK but across nearly all the western world. As Table I.1 shows, in 2000 nearly all the major countries in the West had either moderate left-of-centre governments in power or they were run by coalitions which had strong social democratic components. Now, the situation is completely different. In 2018, of all the countries listed, only Spain and Portugal had recognisably moderate left-of-centre majority governments. With the partial exception of Sweden, which had social democrats still within the governing coalition (although in a comparatively minor role), all the other countries had governments which, by 2018, had swung to the right – in several cases markedly so.

Table I.1: Governments in Europe and North America in 2000 and 2018		
Country	**Government in 2000**	**Government in 2018**
Austria	Social Democrats largest party but with a right-of-centre coalition	Coalition between the moderate and more extreme right
Canada	Liberal Party	Liberal Party
Denmark	Social Democrats	Right-of-centre coalition
Finland	Social Democrats	Right-of-centre coalition
France	Socialist Party-led coalition	En Marche – radical centrist
Germany	Social Democratic Party	Conservative-dominated coalition led by Angela Merkel
Greece	Panhellenic Socialist Movement	Syriza – radical left
Italy	Centre-left coalition	Populist right coalition
Netherlands	Left-of-centre coalition including Dutch Social Democrats	Right-of-centre coalition excluding Dutch Social Democrats
Norway	Labour Party	Right-of-centre coalition
Portugal	Socialist Party	Socialist Party
Spain	Right-of-centre People's Party	Spanish Socialist Workers Party
Sweden	Coalition including the Swedish Social Democrats in a fairly strong position	Coalition with the Social Democrats in a weaker position
UK	Labour Party	Conservative Party supported by the DUP
USA	Democrats yielding to Republicans	Republican

Sources: Wikipedia.

Why should this have happened? Only relatively recently, centre left governance was widely viewed as being almost the natural order of political affairs, especially in stable and relatively prosperous places such as Scandinavia. Many countries had seen the centre left in power for longer than any of their competitors. Why should support for such apparently well-established parties collapse, as has clearly happened? In most cases it was not just that electoral support declined. There were also large falls in party membership. Where this did not happen, as in the case of the UK Labour Party, the section of the US Democratic Party which has supported Bernie Sanders and with Jean-Luc Mélanchon's La France Insoumise, a different phenomenon manifested itself. This has been a marked tendency among left-of-centre supporters and some leaders to move away from the centrist policies generally espoused by the centre left to a resurgence of further left agendas – more public ownership, higher taxes on the rich and a greater role for the state in directing the economy.

There is surely deep significance in the fact that the switch away from social democracy has been so widespread. If only a few countries had seen this happening, it might be plausible to blame it on local circumstances, on leadership failings, and on the unfortunate timing and the outturn of particular events. Clearly, for example, in the UK the Iraq War and the fact that the 2008 crash both occurred on Labour's watch helped the party to lose the 2010 general election. With social democracy suffering such huge reverses across almost the whole of the West over the same period, however, such *ad hoc* explanations lack plausibility. Something much more systematic and fundamental must have gone wrong. The purpose of this book is to explore what this might be in a general international context, but with particular reference to the UK, and then to discuss what might be done to reverse the current decline in the fortunes of the centre left.

It may help at this stage to summarise what this book has to say. Its thesis is that social democratic parties across the western world face major challenges on several different fronts. The first is their poor record, while in government, in achieving reasonably good economic performance from the economies for which they had government responsibility. At the same time, they have been relatively ineffective, when in opposition, at mounting a convincing critique of the poor economic outcomes engineered by non-social democratic governments. On the contrary, their default position has been to agree with the right's austerity agenda, or at least to condone it, while claiming somewhat implausibly to be able to administer it rather more gently, but still effectively.

The main reason for this state of affairs lies in the fact that the centre left has consistently failed to mount a successful counter-attack to the neoliberal overturn of the Keynesian policies which were crucial to the economic success of the immediate post-war period. This policy framework also provided a great deal of credibility to the social democratic governments which were often in charge. The Keynesian consensus fell apart because, when confronted by the inflationary crisis which overtook the world in the 1970s and 1980s, its adherents had no convincing antidote, as they could and potentially should have done. Instead, across the West, the centre left establishment fell in line behind the dominant new monetarist and neoliberal doctrines, although it was always apparent that they served the interests of the right much better than the people whom the left was supposed to be representing.

These problems were made more acute by two other things which happened at more or less the same time. One was that the redistributive agenda, which had always underpinned the centre left's appeal to those on relatively low incomes, became increasingly undermined. One of the major appeals of left-of-centre parties to those relatively low down the income scale has always been the prospect of redistribution of wealth and income in their favour through state action. Those on higher incomes, who believed that a fairer society was worth more than a bit of extra post-tax income in their hands, also wanted to see evidence that any such altruism was worth the candle. As state revenues through taxation and charges bumped up against the UK's tax-take ceiling, and as the gap between those parts of the economy benefitting from globalisation and other changes and those not doing so widened, it became increasingly apparent that the capacity of public expenditure to redistribute income and wealth effectively had been considerably less than most of them hoped it would be.

This development overlapped with another which was that the

Job losses

Immigration?

How many uni educated/voted Labour?

divisions in attitudes and values between different people who
were inclined to support moderate political parties widened as a
result of a combination of globalisation, liberalisation, demographic
changes and slow growth. All helped to increase disparities which
were <u>always</u> going to be there, but which became more acute across
a range of different dimensions. These included gulfs between
those with university education and those without, those living
in metropolitan areas and those in the regions, between people
employed in manufacturing and those in service industries, between
people who had done well out of globalisation and internationalism
and those who had done badly out of them, between baby boomers
and millennials and more generally those who were still getting
richer and those whose incomes had stagnated for year after year.
Culture gaps widened and became more conspicuous, undermining
the <u>cohesion</u> which political parties need to survive, prosper and
win elections.

labour

As a result, the spectrum on which political allegiances lie has
shifted significantly away from the left/right divisions with which
we have for a long time been familiar to something very different.
The new axis might be described as being between nativists and
globalisers. <u>Nativists</u> are cultural conservatives although often
relatively liberal economically. Most of them have stagnant or
declining real incomes. They think that charity starts at home
and that we should be spending most, if not all, of our foreign aid
budget in the UK rather than overseas. Many of them do not have
university degrees, although a lot of them are skilled. They tend to
think that the threat of climate change is exaggerated and are wary
of the high costs of combatting it. They are patriotic and, in the UK
Brexit context, they are quite strongly inclined to favour Leave. They
are supporters of law and order, local communities, trades unions
and traditional values. They favour controls on what they regard
as uncontrolled immigration. They support public expenditure
from which they are beneficiaries but are uncomfortable with
what they regard as a 'nanny state' approach to welfare. They
feel undervalued, under threat and unappreciated. They distrust
the political establishment and resent the fact that much of their
lives seems to be controlled by people with whom they have little

Disproportionally less educated and less support less sentences. Law + order - even though statistically more poorer disproportionally. Rich/well off. prison. (+ most connected/effect) connected?

_?_

+ unchristian values? Racist?

_?_

Selfish?

* Hence Cons Pitch to them. The people v Parliament.
+ why is Labour seen as unpatriotic?
* Trade unions traditional left + Labour?
? * Patriotic xenophobic, Racist?
* Climate change sceptics.

_5_

✶ Europe

affinity, over whom they have little control and for whom they
✶ Corbyn
do not have much respect. They tend to be people who have not
done well out of globalisation and many of them live in parts of the
country which have for a long time been in at least relative decline.

North west— mids·

Globalisers, on the other hand, tend to have opposite views
on all these issues. They tend to have above average incomes
and reasonable prospects of at least slow increases in what they
earn. Most of them are not highly unionised, so their approach
to wage bargaining is individualistic rather than collective. They
have an internationalist outlook, regarding universal problems
such as climate change as being serious challenges to the whole
of humanity. They support foreign aid programmes and welcome
free movement of people and immigration. As regards Brexit, as
internationalists rather than what they would regard as narrow
nationalists, they tend to be for Remain. They are inclined to take
a strongly positive view on issues around race, gender, sexuality
and identity, and to take a liberal and reformist attitude to matters
such as improving the criminal justice system. Broadly speaking
they feel confident and satisfied with their lot in life. Most of them
have good jobs in the service sector for which their education has
given them the qualifications that hold them in good stead. They
tend to be concentrated in major cities, particularly ones with
universities.[1] A major problem for social democrats across the West
is that their parties have been largely taken over by people with
globaliser attitudes to life whereas they depend for a large part of
their electoral support on people with an essentially nativist view
of the world. *ie – working Class*

What can be done? The thesis in this book is that the first and
most crucial way ahead for social democracy is for it to be better
at running the economies for which it might be responsible, and
better at mounting critiques against right-of-centre administrations
which are performing poorly – and therefore relatively harshly,
especially on the most vulnerable – on the economic front. To do
this, the critical requirement is that social democracy breaks free
from some of the key tenets of neoliberalism and embraces policies
which will produce considerably higher rates of economic growth
than we have seen recently. This is not going to be an easy task, but

*what are these policies? Better ct running economies
and critiques in opposition. To produce higher rates
of growth —at cost ♄ environment? Green Policies needed*

the alternative for the moderate left of centre may be something close to extinction.

Second, social democrats need to be better at achieving enough redistribution to stop the divisions in society being as wide as they are now. Public expenditure and the role of the state are inevitably going to continue to be important and the reputation of social democracy for competent and efficient administration is going to remain as crucial as it always has been. This is compatible with a fair amount of redistribution of income from roughly the top 5% to the bottom 20% of income earners. The evidence suggests, however, that whatever the overall benefits of public expenditure may be, achieving much redistribution within the remaining 75% of taxpayers and recipients is never easy, and is made much more difficult if so much of the tax and benefit system is devoted, as it is now, to trying to even up large regional imbalances. Relying on the redistributive powers of taxation and public expenditure to benefit significantly the average C1 or C2 voter, without radical changes in the way the economy is run, is not likely to be successful.

Third, dealing with the disjunction in attitudes and values between globalisers and nativists may turn out to be even more tricky. In countries with proportional representation we can see how nationalist populist parties, reflecting broadly nativist views, have gained a very considerable amount of electoral traction. In the UK, with our first-past-the-post electoral system, getting sufficient numbers of candidates elected at either national or regional level to make any significant electoral inroads is much more difficult. The danger to social democracy, however, is that sufficient numbers of people, who have traditionally voted for the centre left, are drawn to nationalist populist party policies to make social democratic parties unelectable, not least if right-of-centre parties trim their policies to attract nativist floating voters. There are clearly signs of this happening throughout the West.

We turn now to seeing what evidence there is for these propositions and their consequences and, if they are broadly correct, whether it could be possible to recreate something of the political and economic conditions which prevailed across most of the western world in the 1950s and 1960s. These have now slipped from sight as objectives as other parts of the world run their economies very often much better than we do. At the moment, many of the major developing countries appear to have both more social cohesion than much of the West does, combined with incomes per head which may at the moment be well below ours, but might not be for much longer. If more authoritarian regimes grow much faster than those in the West, what may be at stake is not just the future of social democracy but liberal democracy as a whole. If western economies keep on expanding at about 1.5% per annum, which on current trends seems likely, and many of those in the East by 5% a year, or more – all helping to foster hope and optimism among all levels of their populations – the West is indeed going to be challenged. The stakes are very high, and time does not appear to be on our side.

What is more important - in developing countries rise in living standards - even at the cost of. lack of democracy. Happier population easily controlled. Threat to west? Yes if these countries follow an expansionist policy, new colonies? Raw materials -
Collapse of Western Social Cohesion leads to fear of foreign influence. Grist to mill for populist leaders. More insular behaviour evident in Leave vote. Possibly lead to further gains by Authortarian Regimes, Trump Boris, Orban + others. "Strong" politics. Leads to conflict. with China etc. Nationalists never except. close ties with forrisn powers -

1

The embrace of neoliberalism and the decline of economic growth

From 1950 to 1975, the economies of the western world grew by an average of about 4% per annum. During the 25 years from 1975 to 2000, this rate slowed down to around 3% and between 2000 and 2016 it fell to barely 1.5%. This was very different from the experience in most countries in the East, as Table 1.1 shows.

Table 1.1: Average growth rate (%) for selected countries in selected periods			
Country	1950-1975	1975-2000	2000-2016
Canada	4.8	3.0	2.1
China	4.9	7.4	9.3
Eurozone	4.5	2.3	1.2
Japan	8.7	2.8	1.0
South Korea	8.1	7.3	4.1
Norway	3.3	3.3	1.6
Singapore	7.7	7.6	5.2
Switzerland	2.6	1.5	1.8
UK	2.6	2.4	1.8
USA	3.6	3.4	1.9

Sources: *A Millennial Perspective* by Angus Maddison: Paris, OECD 2001 for the years 1950 to 1998, and 2010 and 2018 editions of *International Financial Statistics Yearbook* for the yeas 1999 to 2016.

Current projections, however, suggest that even the poor level of performance achieved recently in the West may not be sustained. If growth rates for the coming years average only, say, 1.5% per annum, as may well be the case in the UK according to forecasts produced by the Office for Budget Responsibility,[1] with similar outcomes elsewhere in the West, the future will look much less promising than it did in years gone by. No longer will it be a reasonable expectation for most people that the years to come will be more prosperous than those in the past, because an overall growth rate of 1.5% per annum is not sufficient to raise the average real income for most of the population. This is the case, particularly where populations are growing fast and the economy is badly balanced, for at least four separate reasons.

One is that population growth – averaging around 400,000 a year recently in the UK[2] – dilutes our GDP per head by about 0.6% per annum. Second, the total available to be paid out as income is further diluted by about £40bn every year as a result of the UK's chronic balance of payments deficits. Third, the share of wages and salaries in GDP is on an inexorable falling trend, because the long-term return on capital – averaging about 2% net of tax – is higher than the close-to-zero rate of real wage increases. Finally, those with sharp elbows tend to secure whatever increases in the income pot might be available, leaving the rest of the population with static or falling living standards.

Furthermore, the coming years may be even more problematic than the decade covering the painfully slow recovery from the 2008 crash. Real incomes for most people are now about the same as they were in 2007 but not significantly lower.[3] This may change for the worse, if significant remedial action is not taken, for there are at least four major calls on GDP in prospect for which, up to now, clearly inadequate provision has been made. If climate change is going to cost us roughly £1trn over the next 30 years, as the government has suggested,[4] this will involve an average annual charge of about 3% per annum on our national income. Increased healthcare expenditure is likely to cost about another 2%, doing something about our current educational standards a further 1% and our ageing population and its associated social care costs at least another 2%. This is 8% in total, representing about 10% of the total 80% of our national income which we currently spend on consumption. We have seen the strains that stagnant incomes put on our social and political fabric. How do we think that real income reductions of as much as 10% for a majority of the population are going to go down?

What went wrong? Why has the growth rate across the whole of the West fallen, when clearly this is not what has been happening in the East – in countries such as China, South Korea and Singapore, whose growth rates are much higher than ours? Why is the West doing so badly?

It is often claimed that there are two main unavoidable reasons for this declining performance, both associated with the relatively high standards of living already attained in the West compared with poorer parts of the world. One is that rising living standards make it increasingly difficult for economies which are already rich to go on getting richer at the same rate as they did before. It has also often been alleged that conditions in the West after World War II were particularly favourable to high growth rates because of demographic changes and technological catch-up following the two World Wars and the slump between them. This, it is argued, may now leave advanced economies short of major technological break-throughs to keep the growth rate up.

Although there is some truth in these contentions, however, neither of them fully captures what has really happened, nor explains how these tendencies might have been offset by better policies. If Singapore can go on growing at 5% per annum or more with a standard of living already much higher than that in nearly all of western Europe, why cannot we do so too?[5]

It is true that as countries get richer they tend to have a falling proportion of their output coming from manufacturing and agriculture, and an increasing share from services. A substantial proportion of this tendency, however, stems from a price effect rather than as a result of changes in relative volumes. Over the last 70 years there has been a dramatic reduction in the real cost of manufactured goods and agricultural products combined with a steady rise in the relative cost of services. These trends have materialised very largely because it has proved to be far easier to increase productivity in manufacturing and agriculture than in services – a recurrent theme in this book. The reason for the slower rate of growth is then the fall in the proportion of GDP coming from manufacturing and agriculture rather than because slower growth is inevitable. The lesson to be drawn from this, however, is not to accept these trends as being unavoidable but to recognise the need for the West to keep a reasonable proportion of its economies engaged in manufacturing. This is the way to avoid major foreign payment deficits and to enable everyone to benefit from the most productive forms of investment, which are typically found in the internationally tradable light industrial sector.

The contention that there are not now enough technological break-throughs to keep advanced economies expanding is equally suspect. This is not only because there is not much sign of technological progress declining but – much more importantly – because most growth does not depend nearly so much on new products being discovered as it does on existing products being produced in larger quantities. The vast majority of human wants and needs could be satisfied by products already produced and sold in the world today, even if there was no further technological progress at all. This is not an argument against research and development, to produce new and better products, and to make production processes generally more efficient. It is simply to point out that growth in output is much less dependent on new products and technical development than most people seem to think it is, and that the notion that the only way to make any economy more competitive and growing faster is by concentrating effort on pushing out the technological frontier is not therefore likely to be successful.

The eclipse of Keynesianism and the break-up of Bretton Woods

If the slowdown in growth in the West has not been caused by an inevitable decline or lack of technological progress, what has been responsible? It has been failure to answer this question satisfactorily which has a lot to do with the decline of social democracy and this is why pinpointing what has really gone wrong is of such key importance.

The thesis of this book is that by far the most important real reason is that the eclipse of Keynesian policies in the 1970s in favour of monetarism and neoliberalism led to new and different economic priorities and incentives being adopted which increasingly unbalanced economies across the West, and pulled down their growth rates. This process made all the countries which adopted these new policies uncompetitive with the East, where policymakers were never captured by the change in policy framework which had swept through the West.

Policies driven by monetarism and neoliberalism, especially very high interest rates, drove up the West's exchange rates compared to those in the East – largely without any serious consideration of the consequences – and made it far cheaper to produce most goods in the East rather than the West. It was a combination of low wages and relatively high productivity, all charged out through the exchange rate at rock-bottom prices, against which the West could not compete. The result has been the precipitate decline of manufacturing as a percentage of GDP in most western countries, the UK being an extreme example. It is this, far more than anything else, which has led to the slowdown in growth across the western world. It is to a large extent because social democracy has had no convincing policies to counter these trends and the near-stagnation which they have produced, that its appeal is so much diminished. One of the key messages in this book is that if social democracy cannot coalesce around a credible growth strategy, it will not recover the huge amount of political support which it has already lost.

It is no coincidence that the much more subdued economic performance across the West after about 1975 than had been achieved during the previous 30 years coincided with the arrival of new economic policies which captured the policymaking scene in the mid-1970s and which have dominated it ever since.

The crucial event which triggered the triumph of monetarism and neoliberalism over the policies pursued during the first 30 years after World War II was the increase in inflation which gripped the world in the 1970s. Keynesian orthodoxy, which had served the world so well in the 1950s and 1960s, had no convincing response to this development. The proximate cause was the break-up in 1971 of the Bretton Woods system, which had provided the framework for world trade and monetary management for the past two and a half decades. On 15th August 1971, the USA, faced with rising balance of payments problems, cut the link between the dollar and the gold at Fort Knox which underpinned it.[6] The result was that all the world currencies became truly fiat based, i.e. depending entirely on the creditworthiness of the governments which issued their currencies, and no longer dependent on gold backing.

Relieved of this constraint, credit was loosened almost everywhere, generating a powerful if short-lived boom. In 1972 the world economy grew by 4.9% and in 1973 by 5.9%.[7] As a result, commodity prices roughly doubled between 1971 and 1973.[8] With their resolve fortified not only by vastly increased demand but also by the outcome of the Yom Kippur War, OPEC, the oil producers' cartel, raised the price of oil from about $2.50 to $10.00 a barrel.[9] With credit creation running out of control, inflation soared everywhere. Year-on-year price increases peaked at 24% in the UK, 14% in the USA, 14% in France, 7% in Germany and – somewhat later than elsewhere – 21% in Italy.[10] Faith in Keynesian demand management withered.

The embrace of monetarist prescriptions

As the certainties of the Bretton Woods and Keynesian world crumbled away, intellectual fashions in economics moved decisively away from the orthodoxy of the previous quarter of a century. Monetarism became the theoretical and practical discipline to which the vast majority of those involved in economic affairs, both in the academic and policymaking worlds, began to subscribe. It is no coincidence, however, that the UK was among the countries which took this shift in policy most seriously. Manufacturing, which was both price sensitive and faced with steeply rising costs charged out to the rest of the world as the exchange rate went up, was bound to suffer from the switch to monetarism. Its leaders already had much less influence than finance, which stood to gain from this new dispensation, at least in the short term.

It was not, however, just the Anglo-Saxon countries with strong classical economic traditions – the UK and the USA – which switched to monetarism and neoliberalism. Similar policies also managed to get their grip on the European Union, leading to the determination, exemplified in the provisions of the 1992 Maastricht Treaty, to put monetary stability before prosperity.[11] The loss of confidence in Keynesian policies after the rising inflation and international dislocation of the 1970s had also caused policy shifts in a monetarist direction, particularly in Germany and France. This change in intellectual fashion, as much as anything else, was responsible for the EU's decline from being one of the world's fastest-growing regions into an area of exceptionally slow increase in output, accompanied by painfully high levels of unemployment.

Countries which have given monetarist prescriptions less priority, on the other hand, both in Europe and elsewhere, continued to grow apace. Norway was a prime example, outside the European Union; although greatly helped by its oil surplus, it achieved the highest rate of GDP per head within the OECD between 1973 and 1992, just ahead of Japan, increasing the population's living standards by over 70%.[12] The Norwegians succeeded in combining this achievement with one of the better OECD records on inflation, with an unemployment rate barely one-third of the then EU average.[13] Over the same period Britain and the USA, both countries strongly influenced by monetarist ideas, achieved GDP per head increases period of only 31% and 26% respectively. The EU chalked up 41%.[14]

Monetarist prescriptions, stripped of their theorising and rhetoric, are familiar to anyone who knows the preconceptions of most of those who make their living out of finance or those with old money fortunes to protect. Their hallmarks are relatively tight money, high real interest rates and the consequently uncompetitive exchange rates which slow down productive enterprise, making it harder to sell abroad and easier to import, discriminating against manufacturing investment, and draining the talent out of industry. Monetarist ideas, and the devotion to balanced budgets and financial conservatism which was its predecessor, harking back to nineteenth-century classical economics, have never been far below the surface, especially in the USA or the UK. Meanwhile the Austrian tradition in economics, with its own strong deflationary bias, held more sway in Germany, buttressed by memories of the hyper-inflation which the Germans had experienced in 1923, in the aftermath of World War I.[15] With these ideas on how to run the economy gaining dominance, post-1973, and especially in the 1980s, it is hardly surprising that increasingly deflationary macro-economic conditions prevailed in both the USA, UK and most of the rest of the western world. They were directly responsible for the low growth and slow productivity increases of the subsequent decades. They also contributed strongly to the huge widening of incomes and wealth which has taken place over the last forty years, with which the attenuation of manufacturing capacity, itself a direct result of monetarist policies, is heavily bound up.

If these policies were so damaging, why were they adopted? Why should a combination of self-interest and social attitudes produce an environment where monetarist ideas could take strong hold even if, as we shall see, they are weak in intellectual coherence and undermined by prescriptive inadequacies – and they have such damaging consequences? Why should mature, stable, slow-growing economies be particularly prone to producing a climate of opinion where such ideas can flourish?

The answer is that the implications of monetarist policies are far from unattractive to large sections of the population, especially in economies already growing relatively slowly, where lenders tend to be in a strong position and borrowers in a weak one. Those who have achieved success in finance rather than manufacturing tend to move into positions of influence and political power. As they do so, the monetarist doctrines which appeal to people with financial backgrounds become increasingly dominant.

The attitudes of those whose business is lending money, who have an obvious stake in high interest rates and scarcity of the commodity they control, become increasingly politically significant, not least because their opinions have a self-fulfilling quality. If there is great fear that losing their confidence will lead to a run on the currency, this places those in a position to keep the parity up by their decisions in a very powerful role. Those whose incomes depend on interest – pensioners and many others – are also naturally inclined to support a policy which seems so obviously in their favour. Bankers, financiers and wealth holders are the immediate beneficiaries of the deflationary policies which follow, buttressed by those who can see no further ahead than obtaining the immediate benefits of low-cost imports and cheap holidays abroad. The losers are those engaged in manufacturing and selling internationally.

The decline and fall of UK manufacturing

When the economy grows slowly, the power and influence of finance increases against that of industry. This is partly a result of the process of accumulation of capital wealth, much of which tends to be invested abroad rather than at home, because slow growth in the domestic economy creates better opportunities overseas. This was the story of Britain in the nineteenth century, the United States for a long period post-World War II, Japan from the 1980s onwards and now China is moving in the same direction. This process produces profound effects on social attitudes and political power, particularly if these conditions prevail for a long period of time, as they have in most of the slow-growing industrialised countries.

If the economy is run with relatively tight money, and high real interest and exchange rates, the inevitable consequence is to produce adverse trading conditions for all output exposed to international competition. Adequate returns on industrial investment are much harder to achieve. It becomes increasingly difficult to pay the going wage or salary rates for the calibre of employees required for success in world markets. Of course, there will always be exceptionally efficient companies, or even industries, such as pharmaceuticals, aerospace and motor vehicle production in the UK, which buck the trend, although it is very significant that these industries do not operate generally in acutely price-sensitive markets.

They are not, however, enough. It is the average which counts, and here the results are impossible to dismiss. The profitability of large sections of manufacturing in the western world has become insufficient for it to be worth-while for them to continue in business. This is why the proportion of GDP derived from manufacturing has fallen so precipitately in most western economies over the last four decades, as the East, particularly along the Pacific Rim, has taken over as the world's new workshop. In 2015 China produced 804m tons of crude steel compared to 166m tons in the whole of the EU and 79m in the USA.[16] In the same year, China produced 24.5m vehicles, Japan – the world leader in the 1970s, '80s and '90s – 9.3m and the USA – the world leader before Japan took over – 12.1m, up from no more than 7.7m. in 2010.[17] The same trends affected swathes of other industries in many other developed economies. Meanwhile, in countries which gave their industrial base a better deal, fortunes were made in manufacturing, and the rest of the economy struggled to keep up.

The most able graduates from western universities nowadays go decreasingly into industry. The easiest money and most glittering careers beckon in the professions, in finance and in the media. The academic world, politics and government service look increasingly more attractive, and for those bent on a career in mainstream business, the service sector generally offers more security and better prospects than manufacturing. If the most able people choose not to go into industry, but instead become lawyers or bankers or television personalities, the educational system responds accordingly.

A significant consequence of the social bias which runs through the whole of this process is that it determines the background of people most likely to reach the peak of their careers running major companies, especially in manufacturing. An interesting contrast between countries such as the USA and Britain, which have grown slowly, and those economies which have grown fastest, is that quite different people tend to become CEOs. In slow-growing economies, chief executives are often professional people such as lawyers and accountants. Where the economy is growing fast, they tend to be engineers and salesmen.

No doubt both cause and effect are operating here. If the most able people in the commercial field are in the professions, they may finish up at the top of big companies, where their talents may be especially in demand to deal with powerful financial interests. In fast-growing economies, where exporting is highly profitable, and where financial considerations are consequently less immediately pressing, engineers and salesmen tend to hold the top positions. It is hardly surprising that companies which are run by accountants and lawyers are particularly concerned with financial results, while those controlled by salesmen and engineers are more orientated to markets and products.

Nor is the low status of industry only a financial or social matter. It also has a large impact on the political weight of manufacturing interests as against those of other parts of the economy. Exercising political power requires talent, takes time and costs money. All are in increasingly short supply particularly in American and British industry, and the results are clear to see. Few members of Congress or Parliament have any significant hands-on manufacturing experience.

The role models to whom the younger generation looks up are nowadays not usually those running manufacturing industries. Those in law practice, accountancy, the media and – at least until recently – investment banking look more impressive and secure. In these circumstances it is small wonder that economic ideas which promote finance over manufacturing tend to find favour. It does not follow, however, that these ideas are well founded. Still less is it true that they are in the best long-term interests of the economy, or even of those in the financial community itself. In the end, those concerned with finance depend as much as everyone else on the performance of the underlying economy, and in particular on its capacity to hold its own in world markets.

The consequences of tight money and high interest rates

The appeal of hard money has a long history and it is – not altogether surprisingly – remarkably resilient. Although monetarism in its more formulaic forms has now largely gone out of fashion, much of the ways of thinking which it promoted – and which still underpin the heavily pro-market, neoliberal approach which has superseded it – are still very widely prevalent. Why, in particular, did social democrats largely accept this policy framework, which has had a lot to do with both the centre left's undoing and the slowing up of growth in most of the West? How did this happen? How did these ideas, despite their inherent weaknesses and baleful consequences, gain such a hold over so many people? What made them so persuasive? And what are their practical implications?

Monetarist and neoliberal views are underpinned by the thinking of a number of key figures, not least those of Professor Friedrich

Hayek (1899-1992) and other associates of Chicago University, who had always had serious reservations about the Keynesian revolution. Monetarist ideas, in their standard form, would not have become accepted as widely as they were, however, without the theoretical and statistical underpinning provided by Milton Friedman (1912-2006) and his associate, Anna Jacobson Schwartz (1915-2012), in their seminal book, *A Monetary History of the United States, 1867–1960*, published in 1963. In this book, they made three important claims which had a major impact on economic thinking all over the world. First, they said that there was a clear association between the total amount of money in circulation and changes in money incomes and prices, but not economic activity, until approximately two years later. Changes in the money supply therefore affected the price level, but not, except perhaps for a short period of time, the level of output in the real economy. Second, these relationships had proved to be stable over a long period. Third, changes (and particularly increases) in the money supply had generally occurred as a result of events which were independent of the needs of the economy. In consequence they added to inflation without raising the level of economic activity.

The attractive simplicity of these propositions is easily recognised. The essence of the monetarist case is that increases in prices and wages not mirrored by productivity increases can be held in check by nothing more complicated than the apparently simple process of controlling the amount of money in circulation. Ideally, a condition of zero inflation is achieved when the increase in the money supply equals the rise in output in the economy. Since both wages and prices can only go up if extra money to finance them is made available, rises in either cannot occur unless more money is provided. Thus, as long as the government is seen to be giving sufficient priority to controlling the money supply, everyone will realise that it is in their interest to exercise restraint, reducing the rate of inflation to whatever level is deemed acceptable.

Especially at a time of unprecedently high levels of inflation, it is understandable that these prescriptions attracted much support to the monetarist banner, although it had always been clear that its intellectual underpinning had severe deficiencies.

To start with, the theory begged the fundamental question as to the appropriate way to measure the money stock when so many different ways of determining it were available. It was, as widely recognised, that the ratio between the stock of money, however defined, and the volume of transactions could vary widely, as the so-called 'velocity of circulation' altered. In addition, there has been widespread criticism of the methodology used by Friedman and Schwartz in their analysis of the relationship between money and prices in the USA, indicating that the statistical basis from which their conclusions were drawn was not nearly as sound as they claimed it was.[18]

As with so much else in economics, there is a major feedback problem with much of the monetarist position, making it difficult to distinguish between cause and effect. It may be true that over a long period the total amount of money in circulation bears a close relationship to the total value of the economy's output. It does not follow, however, that the money supply determines the money value of GDP, and hence the rate of inflation. It may well be, instead, that the total amount of money in circulation is a function of the need for sufficient finance to accommodate transactions. If this is so, then an increase in the money supply may well accompany an increase in inflation caused by some other event, simply to provide this accommodation. It need not necessarily be the cause of rising prices at all.

Common sense tells us that changes in the money supply are only one of a number of relevant factors determining rises or falls in inflation. Monetarists, however, rejected this proposition, alleging that all alterations in the rate of price increases are caused by changes in the money supply some two years previously. They also claimed that the future course of inflation could be guided within narrow limits by controlling the money stock. Empirical evidence demonstrates that this contention is far too precise, and greatly overstates the predictive accuracy of monetarist theories.

For this amount of fine tuning to be possible, an unequivocal definition of money is required. It is one thing to recognise a situation where clearly far too much money, or, more accurately, too much credit is being created. Monetarists are right in saying

21

that if credit is so cheap and so readily available that it is easy to speculate on asset inflation, or the economy is getting overheated by excess demand financed by excessive credit creation, then the money supply is too large. This is a broad quantitative judgement. It is quite another matter to state that small alterations in the money supply generate correspondingly exact changes in the rate of inflation. Yet this is the claim which monetarists put forward.

The failings in monetarist theory

This claim is implausible for a number of reasons. One is the difficulty, already referred to, in defining accurately what is money and what is not. Notes and coins are clearly 'money', but where should the line be drawn thereafter? What kinds of bank facilities and money market instruments should also be included or excluded? Many different measures are available in every country, depending on what is put in and what is left out. None of them has been found anywhere to have had a strikingly close correlation with subsequent changes in the rate of inflation for any length of time. Often, different measures of the money supply move in different directions. This is very damaging evidence against propositions which are supposed to be precise in their formulation and impact.

Another major problem for monetarists, referred to above, is that there can be no constant ratio between the amount of money in circulation, however defined, and the aggregate value of transactions, because the rate at which money circulates can, and does, vary widely over time. The 'velocity of circulation', which is the ratio between the GDP and the money supply, is indeed far from constant. In the USA the M3 velocity fell 17% between 1970 and 1986, but by 1996 it had risen 22% compared to ten years earlier. It has been exceptionally volatile in Britain, where it rose by 7% between 1964 and 1970, and by a further 28% between 1970 and 1974, only to fall by 26% between 1974 and 1979.[19] Other countries, such as the Netherlands and Greece, have also had large changes in the velocity of circulation, particularly during the 1970s.[20] More recently there have been huge increases in the money supply in relation to GDP, implying very substantial reductions in the velocity of circulation. In the USA, for example, M2 rose 79%[21] between 2000 and 2010 while the economy grew in money terms by no more than 49%.[22]

Some of these movements were caused by changes in monetary policy, but a substantial proportion, especially recently, have had nothing to do with the government. They have been the results of radical changes to the financial environment, caused by the effects of deregulation on credit creation, and the growth of new financial instruments, such as derivatives. Variations like this make it impossible to believe in the rigid relationship that monetarism requires. In fact, the statistical record everywhere on the money supply and inflation shows what one would expect if there was very little causation at all at work. Except in extreme circumstances of gross over-creation of money and credit, changes in the money supply have had little or no impact on the rate of inflation. The need to provide enough money to finance all the transactions taking place has, over the long term, proved to be much more important a determinant of the money supply than attempts to restrict it to control inflation, although some countries have certainly had tighter monetary policies than others. In the short term, there is no systematic evidence that changes in the money supply affect subsequent inflation rates with any precision at all.

It is not surprising, therefore, that the predictions of monetarists about future levels of inflation, based on trends in the money supply, have turned out to be no better, and often worse, than those of other people who have used more eclectic, common-sense methods. Monetarists have not kept their predictions, however, solely to the future rate of inflation. There are three other areas of economic policy where their ideas have had a decisive effect on practical policy over the last forty years, shaping the way in which governments of all political persuasions in the UK and elsewhere have approached economic policy formation. These are to do with unemployment, interest rates and exchange rates. Pure monetarism may have faded from fashion but it has left a very powerful and durable legacy in these key policy areas.

The monetarist – now shading into the neoliberal – view of unemployment is that there is a 'natural' rate which cannot be avoided, set essentially by supply-side rigidities. Any attempt to reduce unemployment below this level by reflation will necessarily increase wage rates and then the price level. This will leave those in employment no better off than they were before, while the increased demand, having been absorbed by higher prices, will result in the same number of people being employed as previously. Increasing demand only pushes up the rate of inflation. It will not raise either output or the number of people in work.

At some point, as pressure on the available labour force increases and the number of the unemployed falls, there is no doubt that a bidding up process will take place, and wages and salaries will rise. This is an altogether different matter, however, from postulating that unemployment levels like those seen over much of the developed world during the 1980s are required to keep inflation at bay. Nor is it plausible that supply side rigidities are the major constraint on getting unemployment down. There is no evidence that these rigidities are significantly greater now than they were in the 1950s and 1960s, and on balance they are almost certainly less. If, during the whole of these two decades, it was possible to combine high rates of economic growth with low levels of unemployment, while inflation remained reasonably stable at an acceptable level, why should we believe that it is impossible now for these conditions to prevail again?

Monetarism also had a considerable influence on interest rates, particularly during the 1980s. The tight control of the money supply which monetarists advocated then could only be achieved if interest rates were used to balance a relatively low supply of money against the demand for credit which had to be choked off by raising the price of money. This requirement was made to seem less harsh by suggesting that a positive rate of interest would always be required to enable lenders to continue providing money to borrowers. It was alleged that any attempt to lower interest rates to encourage expansion would fail as lenders withdraw from the market until the premium they required above the inflation rate reappeared.

Yet again, we have a proposition much more strongly based on assertion than on evidence, especially in the light of recent experience. For years on end, in many countries, real interest rates paid to savers have been negative, sometimes even before tax. Lenders, of course, have never regarded negative interest rates as fair, and frequently complain bitterly when they occur. There is, however, little that they can do about them. Their ability to withdraw from the market is generally limited. It is undoubtedly the case, however, that high positive rates of interest are a discouragement to investment, partly directly, but much more importantly, because of their influence on driving up the exchange rate.

The neglect of exchange rate policy

This is particularly paradoxical in relation to the third major impact of monetarist ideas on practical issues, which has been on exchange rate policy. Monetarists have always argued that no policy for improving an economy's competitiveness by devaluation will work, because the inflationary effects of a depreciation will automatically raise the domestic price level back to where it was in international terms. This will leave the devaluing country with no more competitiveness than it had before, but with a real extra inflationary problem with which it will have to contend.

This proposition, which is still widely believed, is one which it is easy to test against historical experience. There have been large numbers of substantial exchange rate changes over the last few decades, providing plenty of empirical data against which to assess the validity of this monetarist assertion. The evidence, as is amply demonstrated by Table 1.2, is overwhelmingly against it. There is example after example to be found of devaluations failing to produce sufficient excess inflation, if any, to wipe out the competitive advantage initially gained. On the contrary, there is ample evidence indicating that exactly the opposite effect has been the experience in a wide variety of different economies.

Those which have devalued have tended to perform progressively better, as their manufacturing sectors expanded, and the internationally tradable goods and services which they produced became cumulatively more competitive.

Table 1.2: Exchange rate changes, consumer prices, the real wage, GDP, industrial output and employment (Year-on-year percentage changes except for unemployment)

	Year	Consumer prices	Wage rates	Real wage change	GDP change	Industrial output change	Unemployment (%)
Britain – 31%	1930	–6.0	–0.7	5.3	–0.7	–1.4	11.2
devaluation against	1931	–5.7	–2.1	3.6	–5.1	–3.6	15.1
the dollar and 24%	1932	–3.3	–1.7	1.6	0.8	0.3	15.6
against all currencies	1933	0.0	–0.1	–0.1	2.9	4.0	14.1
in 1931	1934	0.0	1.5	1.5	6.6	5.5	11.9
France – 27%	1956	2.0	9.7	7.7	5.1	9.4	1.1
devaluation	1957	3.5	8.2	4.7	6.0	8.3	0.8
against all	1958	15.1	12.3	–2.8	2.5	4.5	0.9
currencies in	1959	6.2	6.8	0.6	2.9	3.3	1.3
1957-58	1960	3.5	6.3	2.8	7.0	10.1	1.2
	1961	3.3	9.6	6.3	5.5	4.8	1.1
USA – 28%	1984	4.3	4.0	–0.3	6.2	11.3	7.4
devaluation	1985	3.6	3.9	0.3	3.2	2.0	7.1
against all	1986	1.9	2.0	0.1	2.9	1.0	6.9
currencies over	1987	3.7	1.8	–1.9	3.1	3.7	6.1
1985-87	1988	4.0	2.8	–1.2	3.9	5.3	5.4
	1989	5.0	2.9	–2.1	2.5	2.6	5.2
Japan – 47%	1989	2.3	3.1	0.8	4.8	5.8	2.3
revaluation	1990	3.1	3.8	0.7	4.8	4.1	2.1
against all	1991	3.3	3.4	0.1	4.3	1.8	2.1
currencies over	1992	1.7	2.1	0.4	1.4	–6.1	2.2
1990-94	1993	1.3	2.1	0.8	0.1	–4.6	2.5
	1994	0.7	2.3	1.6	0.6	0.7	2.9
Italy – 20%	1990	6.4	7.3	0.9	2.1	–0.6	9.1
devaluation	1991	6.3	9.8	3.5	1.3	–2.2	8.6
against all	1992	5.2	5.4	0.2	0.9	–0.6	9.0
currencies over	1993	4.5	3.8	–0.7	–1.2	–2.9	10.3
1990-93	1994	4.0	3.5	–0.5	2.2	5.6	11.4
	1995	5.4	3.1	–2.3	2.9	5.4	11.9
Finland – 24%	1990	6.1	9.4	3.3	0.0	–0.1	3.5
devaluation	1991	4.1	6.4	2.3	–7.1	–9.7	7.6
against all	1992	2.6	3.8	1.2	–3.6	2.2	13.0
currencies over	1993	2.1	3.7	1.6	–1.6	5.5	17.5
1991-93	1994	1.1	7.4	6.3	4.5	10.5	17.4
	1995	1.0	4.7	3.7	5.1	7.8	16.2
Spain – 18%	1991	5.9	8.2	2.3	2.3	–0.7	16.3
devaluation	1992	5.9	7.7	1.8	0.7	–3.2	18.5
against all	1993	4.6	6.8	2.2	–1.2	–4.4	22.8
currencies over	1994	4.7	4.5	–0.2	2.1	7.5	24.1
1992-94	1995	4.7	4.8	0.1	2.8	4.7	22.9
	1996	3.6	4.8	1.2	2.2	–0.7	22.2
Britain – 19%	1990	9.5	9.7	0.2	0.6	–0.4	6.8
devaluation	1991	5.9	7.8	1.9	–1.5	–3.3	8.4
against all	1992	3.7	11.3	7.6	0.1	0.3	9.7
currencies	1993	1.6	3.2	1.6	2.3	2.2	10.3
in 1992	1994	2.4	3.6	1.2	4.4	5.4	9.6
	1995	3.5	3.1	–0.4	2.8	1.7	8.6
Argentina – 72%	2000	–0.9	1.2	3.3	–0.8	–0.3	14.7
devaluation	2001	–1.1	–2.6	–23.3	–4.4	–7.6	18.1
against all	2002	25.9	1.9	–11.5	–10.9	–10.5	17.5
currencies	2004	13.4	17.6	8.8	16.2	16.8	
early 2002	2004	4.4	13.7	9.0	10.7	13.6	
	2005	9.6	22.8	11.9	9.2	8.5	8.7
Iceland – 50%	2005	4.0	6.3	2.3	7.2	12.4	2.6
devaluation	2006	6.7	8.8	2.1	4.7	16.8	2.9
against all	2007	5.1	9.8	4.7	6.0	0.7	2.3
currencies	2008	12.7	8.5	–4.2	1.2	35.5	3.0
2007-09	2009	12.0	3.0	–9.0	–6.6	3.8	7.2
	2010	5.4	6.1	0.7	–4.0	10.6	7.6
	2011	4.0	7.1	3.1	2.6	13.5	7.0

Sources: *Economic Statistics 1900-1983* by Thelma Liesner. London: *The Economist* 1985. IMF *International Financial Statistics Yearbooks,* Eurostatistics and British, Argentine and Icelandic official statistics and International Labour Organisation tables.

Countries which have gained an initial price advantage therefore tend to forge ahead, with increasingly competitive import-saving and exporting sectors. Rapidly growing efficiency in the sectors of their economies involved in international trading gains them higher shares in world trade, providing them with platforms for further expansion. High productivity growth generates conditions which may even allow them, with good management, to experience less domestic inflation that their more sluggish competitors. In practice, monetarist policies have had pronounced effects on the exchange rates of the countries where they have been most effectively imposed, but invariably their impact has been to push them up. The economies concerned then suffer the worst of all worlds – an all too familiar mixture of unimpressive growth, low increases in output to absorb wage and salary increases, and sometimes higher price inflation than their more favoured competitors.

Conclusion

Monetarist theories – and neoliberalism – start by appearing simple and straightforward, but end by being long on complication and assertion, and short on predictive and practical prescriptive qualities. They pander to the prejudice of those who would like to believe their conclusions. They lack convincing explanations about the transmission mechanisms between what they claim are the causes of economic events, and the effects which they declare will necessarily follow. Where they can be tested against empirical results, the predictions their theories produce generally fail to achieve levels of accuracy which make them worthwhile. This is why monetarism in its purer forms is no longer fashionable.

Monetarist theories, and the neoliberalism which has flowed from them, have nevertheless reinforced everywhere all the prejudices widely held in favour of the cautious financial conservatism, which monetarism and neoliberalism so accurately reflect. In this key respect, these ideas still have a very powerful influence on current policy-making. By allowing themselves to be persuaded by these misguided doctrines, it becomes all too easy for those responsible for running the nation's affairs to acquiesce in accepting levels of low growth and under-employment which would never have been tolerated if everyone had realised how unnecessary they were. The result has been that policies which should have been rejected have continued to be accepted, although they failed to work. Because expectations have been lowered, the deflationary consequences of high real interest rates, restrictive monetary policies and overvalued exchange rates have not caused the outcry that might have been expected, and which they deserved.

We turn now to what neoliberal policies have done to unbalance the economies which have been subject to them, concentrating on the UK experience, although this is mirrored in varying degrees across all the western world. It is then possible to see how uncritical adherence to these policies has done more than anything else to undermine the electoral attractions of the centre left, and to leave social democrats losing elections.

2

The UK's unbalanced economy

The UK economy has grown much more slowly recently than it has done in the past because the way in which it has been run, particularly during the period since the 1970s, has left it extraordinarily unbalanced in a number of key respects.

Investment in the UK, for a start, currently accounts for just over 16% of GDP according to the Office for National Statistics (ONS)[1] (or 17% in IMF publications)[2] compared with a world average of 26% and about 45% in China.[3] The figure of 16% – which was 19% as late as 2008[4] – includes investment in intangibles which the ONS designates as 'intellectual property'. Excluding this component, tangible investment accounts for no more than just over 13% of GDP.[5] As depreciation is running at almost the same rate,[6] after taking this into account, practically nothing is left. Further analysis shows the situation to be even worse than these total figures might suggest. In particular, investment in 'Other machinery and equipment', which covers the most highly productive forms of investment in terms of productivity growth, has fallen by more than 25% as a percentage of GDP – from 4.0% in 2008 to 2.9% in 2018.[7]

This is by far the most important reason why productivity in the UK is virtually static, particularly when the key characteristics of different types of investment are taken into account. Some types of investment have a much larger impact on the growth rate than others. In particular, there are three – mechanisation, technology and power – whose emerging salience 250 years ago provided the foundation for the Industrial Revolution, generating much faster economic growth than had ever been seen before. Their key characteristic is their ability vastly to increase output per hour, typified by a bulldozer replacing a shovel, a computer being used instead of a multiplication table, a lorry/truck being employed instead of a wheelbarrow, a combine harvester replacing a sickle, or a new machine being installed which produces a multiple per hour of the products compared to the one it replaces. The benefits derived from investment of this type are then diffused through the economy as higher output, increased wages, better and cheaper products, greater profits, and a larger tax base – all building up to produce an exceptionally high total social (as opposed to just a private) rate of return.

A classic example may help to make the point. In 1500 about 60% of the UK labour force was employed in agriculture. By 1700 this ratio had fallen to about 20%[8]. By 1850 it was barely 20% and it is now 1.5%, and still producing about 60% of all our food.[9] The massive increases in productivity captured by these figures was achieved by key combinations of technology, mechanisation and power. By contrast, it still takes the same amount of time now as it did 500, 300, or 150 years ago to cut someone's hair or to serve him or her with a meal. In agriculture's case productivity has increased by a factor of thousands of percent. In the archetypical service examples of haircuts and serving meals there has been no increase in productivity at all.

Poor investment and low social rates of return

The social rate of return – which measures productivity increases – is defined here as the ratio, calculated over a reasonable length of time, between the increase in GDP and gross expenditure on investment over the same period. Gross investment as a percentage of GDP multiplied by the social rate of return, as an accounting identity, then equals the average growth rate. Total returns to the economy from different types of investment can then be quantified. However important it is in social terms, most public-sector investment – in road, rail, schools, hospitals, public facilities and housing – has a low social rate of return and does not contribute much to increases in GDP. The same is true of much private sector investment – in office blocks, shopping centres, new restaurants and at least some IT installations. Mechanisation, technology and power, on the other hand, can produce much higher social rates of return, typically running at 50% per annum or even more.

Table 2.1: Gross investment, social rates of return and growth rates, for selected countries and selected periods.

Country	Period	Gross investment as a % of GDP	Average social rate of return	Average growth rate
UK	1934-1941	13%	46%	6.0%
USA*	1939-1944	7%	144%	10.1%
Japan	1953-1970	29%	35%	10.1%
China	2002-2012	37%	25%	9.1%
South Korea	2005-2016	30%	12%	3.5%
Singapore	2005-2016	26%	20%	5.3%
UK	2005-2016	17%	8%	1.4%
World	2005-2016	26%	14%	3.5%

*The Gross Investment figure for the USA for the period 1939 to 1944 covers private investment only, so the average social rate of return for the US economy must have been lower than 164%.

Evidence that much higher social rates of return can be achieved than those being currently achieved in the UK is readily available. To take some extreme examples, illustrated in Table 2.1, Japan achieved a 35% average annual social rate of return on all its gross investment for the whole of the period 1953 to 1970, with physical investment accounting for just under 30% of GDP.[10] No wonder the Japanese economy expanded by 10% per annum cumulatively over these two decades. The USA had an extraordinary period between 1939 and 1944 during which its economy doubled in size.[11] This was achieved because relatively modest amounts of investment – heavily concentrated in manufacturing to support the war effort – produced an average social rate of return which appears to have been in excess of 100%.[12] The UK also had a golden period from 1934 to 1941 as rearmament drove GDP up at the same time as the economy picked up the slack left from the slump. During this period the average social rate of return was 46%, with 13% of GDP devoted to physical investment, producing a cumulative average annual growth rate between 1934 and 1941 of 6.0% – including a staggeringly high increase of 16% just between 1939 and 1940 – a much better growth performance than has been seen at any time before or since.[13]

Moving to more recent times, the huge recent expansion in the Chinese economy has been driven by both high social rates of return and a high proportion of GDP being devoted to investment. Over the period between 2002 to 2012, China's social rate of return averaged 25% while the proportion of GDP devoted to investment averaged 37%,[14] producing a cumulative growth rate of over 9% per annum. Also showing what can be done by a much richer economy, between 2005 and 2016 the Singaporean economy grew cumulatively by 5.3% per annum with a social rate of return of 20% and 26% of GDP accounting for investment.[15] South Korea, by contrast, grew over the same period by an average of 3.5% per annum with a social rate of return of no more than 12% but with 30% of GDP going into investment.[16] At the same time growth in the UK averaged 1.4% per annum, the social rate of return was 8% and the proportion of GDP devoted to investment, including IP, was 17%, falling to barely 12% if IP is excluded.[17]

Measurements of total gross investment inevitably include large outlays on types of investment which self-evidently we know have low social rates of return. Furthermore, gross investment figures take no account of depreciation. It is impossible, therefore, to avoid the conclusion that, to achieve the average figure that the statistics show, in the right circumstances the social rate of return on the most productive new investment must be comfortably in the 50% per annum region – and higher still in the most favourable cases.

Most of the investment which has these very high-powered characteristics tends to be found in the private rather than the public sector, some of it in services but pre-eminently in light industry whose output is internationally traded. It will therefore only materialise if there is a reasonable chance of it being profitable. The problem in the UK is that the exchange rate has for many decades been much too high for this condition to be fulfilled. This is why we have deindustrialised to the extent we have.

Figure 2.1 shows movements in the real exchange rate between the UK and China – which is a reasonable proxy for what has happened between most of the West and most of the East over recent decades. The UK economy was none too competitive in the late 1970s when the advent of monetarism, then morphing into neoliberalism, hugely raised interest rates, with base rates –

let alone market rates – peaking at 17% in November 1979, with another peak of 15% in October 1989.[18] The exchange rate rose by over 60% in real terms between 1977 and 1982[19] as the battle to control inflation took centre stage, while any collateral impact on UK competitiveness of the policies adopted to control price rises was simply ignored.

Worse, however, was to follow. After some respite after 1992, when the UK fell out of the EU's Exchange Rate Mechanism (ERM), sterling strengthened again as capital movements were liberalised – and encouraged – to an extent unrivalled anywhere else in the world. The result was a huge capital inflow as vast swathes of the UK economy – our ports, airports, energy companies, utilities, football clubs, large sections of what was left of our manufacturing base, and much else – were sold to foreign interests. Between 2000 and 2010 net sales overseas of UK portfolio assets – shares in existing companies, bonds and property but excluding direct investment in buildings and machinery – are reported by the ONS to have totalled £615bn.[20] No wonder that, as a result, the pound soared again until by 2007 it was worth more than $2.00.[21]

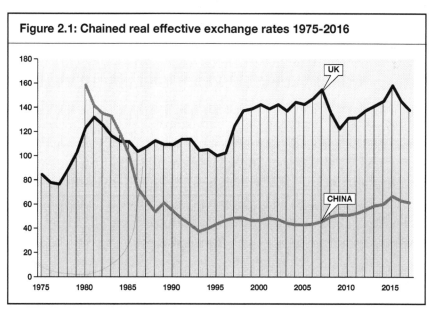

Figure 2.1: Chained real effective exchange rates 1975-2016

Sources: International Financial Statistics Yearbooks. Washington DC, IMF. 2000 edition: pages 344 & 345 for China and 980 & 981 for the UK; 2010 edition: page 229 for China and 744 for the UK; 2018 edition: page 279 for China and 1055 for the UK. Based in all cases on relative unit labour costs.

Because the world market for manufactured goods is very competitive, it is hardly surprising that UK industry reeled under this onslaught. On average, about one third of total manufacturing costs consist of machinery, raw materials and components, for which there are generally world prices.[22] The other two-thirds of charges – for direct labour, management and all other overhead costs including interest and a provision for taxation – are incurred in sterling and the rate at which they are charged out to the rest of the world is directly reflected in the exchange rate. As a first approximation, therefore, and as an example, the 60% increase in the real exchange rate in the late 1970s and early 1980s added two-thirds of 60% (i.e. 40%) to the underlying costs of UK exports, while making imports correspondingly cheaper.

Concern over the decline of manufacturing in the UK has a long history although the many reports which have been produced to remedy matters have turned out – almost without exception – to be ineffective, with consequences of our poor economic performance often being misdiagnosed as the causes of it. Broadly speaking the left has favoured state intervention on such matters as improving education and training, making finance more readily available to industry, changing company governance to reduce 'short-termism' and increasing public expenditure to improve the infrastructure. The right, on the other hand, has favoured more competition, lower taxes, privatisation, deregulation and a smaller state. While both these approaches may have some merit in appropriate circumstances, there is little evidence that, on their own, any of these policies would make a material positive difference to the performance of the economy. The reason is that none of them gets to the core problem which is that, unless investment in the private sector is likely to be profitable, it will not be undertaken by businesses which need to make a profit to survive.

If we are going to get the economy to grow more rapidly, therefore, we need to change the economic incentives available to both existing companies and to new entrants. We have to make investment, especially of the high-powered types, profitable enough to attract resources, so that we can make it materialise on a much larger scale than it is now in the UK. If this can be done, however, the prospects for lifting the growth rate from 1.5% to, say, 3.5% become much more promising. Essentially what needs to be done is very simple. It is to shift around 4% of our GDP out of consumption and into investment with a 50% social rate of return. 4% x 50% provides the 2% difference between 1.5% and 3.5% growth per annum.

The imbalance between manufacturing and services

The second major imbalance in the UK economy is that our manufacturing base has been allowed to decline to an extent which is greater than what has happened to any other major developed nation. It is true that there is a tendency for all advanced economies to see their service sectors expanding at the expense of manufacturing. This is, of course, partly a price effect as the cost of manufactured goods falls while those of services rise. It is also the case that the borderline between manufacturing and services is sometimes blurred. Making full allowance for all these factors, however, does not alter the fact that the UK has deindustrialised to a much greater extent than any other developed country. Even as late as 1970, about 32% of UK GDP came from manufacturing.[23] Now the percentage is 9.7% and still slipping downwards.[24] The extreme case of deindustrialisation from which the UK suffers is a major drawback for the economy for at least four separate but overlapping reasons.

Table 2.2: Growth, manufacturing and investment as a percentage of GDP in various countries.

	China	Korea	Singapore	Germany	Holland	USA	UK
Growth in GDP 2006-2016	136%	39%	59%	19%	9%	14%	12%
Growth in population 2006/16	5.6%	3.9%	21.9%	0.5%	3.3%	8.2%	8.2%
Growth in GDP per head 2006/16	124%	33%	30%	19%	6%	5%	3%
Manufacturing as a % of GDP	29%	29%	20%	23%	12%	12%	10%
Investment as a % of GDP	45%	29%	27%	19%	19%	20%	17%

Sources: Various tables in *International Monetary Statistics Yearbook 2017*. Washington DC: IMF, 2017. Manufacturing data from the World Bank website. This data relates to 2016 as does the IMF data on Investment as a % of GDP.

The first is that productivity increases are much easier to achieve in manufacturing than they are in services, so the smaller manufacturing is as a percentage of GDP, the lower the growth rate is likely to be. Table 2.2 shows the high correlation there is across a range of economies between those which have strong manufacturing sectors and relatively high growth rates and those that do not do so. The major reason why productivity growth tends to be higher in light industry is because mechanisation, technology and power, the most productive forms of investment in terms of added output per hour, tend to find a natural home in this part of the economy.

The second reason why manufacturing is so important is that it provides regions of the UK outside the South East of England with output to sell, so that they can pay their way. At present, large swathes of the UK run huge deficits with the rest of the world. If London runs a balance of payments surplus of something like £50bn a year, which a relatively recent (2013) Greater London Authority (GLA) report indicated that it does[25], the rest of the country has to share out the UK's balance of payments deficit, which has recently been running close to £100bn a year. This means that perhaps three quarters of the economy – about £1.5bn per annum in total turnover – is sharing out a deficit which is as high as £150bn, implying that about three quarters of the UK is running at an average deficit of something like 10%. Clearly some cities outside London – Oxford, Cambridge and Bristol, for example – are doing reasonably well in terms of paying their way, but this only means that the rest of the country is doing even worse than the 10% deficit average. No wonder that there are such huge disparities in gross value added (GVA) per employee as the statistics show: an average in 2017 of £49k in London, just under £20k in Wales and just over £20k in the North East.[26]

Third, there is substantial evidence that, on balance, manufacturing employment provides a more satisfying job environment than much service-sector employment. This is partly because there may be intrinsic satisfaction to be gained from making things but also because the pattern of employment in manufacturing tends to be more evenly spread across skill and ability levels than in services, which are more inclined to produce large numbers of jobs which are either highly skilled or relatively unskilled, with a gap in the middle. Despite the cavalier way in which manufacturing has been treated in the UK, average wages there are still substantially higher than they are on average in services – with a gap in manufacturing's favour currently running at almost 20%.[27]

Finally, producing manufactured goods is key to the ability of the UK – or any other advanced and diversified economy – to pay its way in the world. Because our manufacturing base is so weak, we have a very large deficit on goods – £135bn in 2017,[28] of which £98bn was manufactures.[29] Although the UK does well on net export of services, with a surplus in 2017 of £107bn, this still left a substantial trade deficit gap of £29bn, contributing to our next major problem, which is our balance of payments deficit.

Deteriorating balance of payments

On its own, a trade deficit of around £30bn for an economy with total GDP of approximately £2trn should not be too big a problem. Unfortunately, however, as Table 2.3 shows, the UK's foreign payments position is much weaker than our trade deficit on its own would imply. We are in this position because of two other major factors.

One is that we have a large and increasingly negative net income from abroad. As recently as 2011, we had a surplus, but the balance has deteriorated sharply since then, the underlying reason being that every year we have a current account deficit we have to borrow from abroad or to sell assets to foreign interests to finance the deficiency. All the time we do so, the interest and profit remittances we have to pay abroad go up, increasing our negative net income from overseas. The other additional burden on our balance of payments deficit is in the form of net transfers abroad. About half of these are net payments to the European Union, with the remainder being split roughly equally between net remittances abroad by immigrants to the UK, and the cost across the exchanges of our aid programmes.

Table 2.3: UK balance of payments breakdown (all figures in £bn)

Year	Goods balance	Services balance	Trade balance	Net income	Net transfers	Balance of payments
2007	−88.6	53.6	−35.0	−7.2	13.1	−55.3
2008	−91.7	52.7	−39.0	−14.6	−13.2	−66.8
2009	−85.3	57.0	−28.3	−11.5	−14.8	−54.6
2010	−95.6	60.5	−35.1	1.1	−19.6	−53.6
2011	−94.4	75.9	−18.5	6.5	−20.3	−32.2
2012	−106.7	81.1	−25.6	−17.8	−20.4	−63.8
2013	−119.0	90.0	−29.0	−36.4	−25.3	−90.7
2014	−122.1	92.4	−29.7	−37.8	−23.4	−90.9
2015	−117.8	90.8	−27.0	−43.0	−23.2	−93.2
2016	−132.7	101.8	−30.9	−49.4	−22.5	−102.8
2017	−137.0	113.1	−23.9	−23.6	−20.9	−68.4
2018	−138.1	107.1	−31.0	−26.7	−24.0	−81.6

Source: Time Series Dataset. London: ONS, June 2019

It is simply unsustainable for the UK to continue indefinitely running a balance of payments deficit every year of anything close to £100bn, which is roughly 5% of our GDP.[30] The rest of the world is not going to support for ever the British people enjoying a standard of living up to 5% higher than they are earning. Sooner or later, the markets are going to realise that the current dispensation cannot last, and that sterling will have to become weaker to take the strain. We need to catch this situation and to take advantage of it before we get forced into a damaging and pointless retreat, while the defensive action we take to keep the pound stronger than it should be means years more of harmful and unnecessary austerity and low growth.

Two other issues to do with our balance of payments deficit are worth highlighting. One is that all our deficit and more is with the EU27[31] and not – in aggregate – with the rest of the world, where we have a small surplus.[32] Although it does not really matter with which countries we have a surplus or a deficit if the total balances are within tolerable limits, the fact that all our foreign payments deficit is with the EU27 is clearly a factor which ought to bear on our current Brexit negotiations, although this important topic is barely – if ever – mentioned. The other is that the exchange rate has a big influence on the size of the net income from abroad element of our deficit. The stronger sterling is, the larger the sterling returns from the UK economy to foreigners become and the smaller is the sterling value of total profit remittances and interest payments from abroad. A weaker pound would thus not only make our exports more competitive and reduce import penetration. It would also reduce the scale of our negative net income from abroad.

Too much borrowing

There has been a staggeringly large increase in debt within the UK economy since the turn of the current century. By 2016 the total monetary base in the UK economy had grown to almost 15 times the size it had been in 2000[33] – a period when the economy grew in real terms by no more than 32%.[34] There are two interlocking reasons why this has happened, and both involve heavy distortions and mismanagement in the way the UK economy is structured.

Table 2.4: UK net lending (+) and net borrowing (–) by sector (in £bn)					
Year	Public sector	Corpora-tions	House-holds	Rest of the world	Totals
2008	–81.4	–13.4	29,2	66.5	1.0
2009	–155.0	19.1	81.6	54.4	0.2
2010	–147.3	10.2	83.4	54.3	0.7
2011	–122.9	32.4	57.7	33.0	0.2
2012	–136.8	11.1	62.6	64.4	1.3
2013	–94.0	–42.5	44.9	91.9	0.3
2015	–79.6	–73.0	59.2	95.1	1.7
2016	–57.0	–62.5	16.8	104.5	1.9
2017	–37.6	–16.2	–24.4	70.1	–8.1
2018	–32.7	–42.5	–20.6	84.1	–11.6

Source: Time Series data supporting ONS Quarterly National Accounts 2018 Q4. London: ONS, June 2019. Figures for 2017 and 2018 are still being reconciled by ONS and the net totals will also be at or very close to zero when this process is complete.

The first is that over the years since 2000, the UK has sustained balance of payments deficits – usually large ones – almost every year. The total accumulated deficit between 2000 and 2017 came to just over £1trn.[35] Table 2.4 shows how this impacted on borrowing and lending within the UK economy between the more recent years 2008 to 2017.

The crucial take from this table is that it highlights that all borrowing and all lending – and all surpluses and all deficits – have, as an accounting identity, to sum to zero. Unless completely implausible assumptions are made about borrowing and lending by corporations and households, a substantial balance of payments deficit – represented in this context by lending to the UK from the rest of the world – is therefore bound to leave the government with a large deficit. This is exactly what has happened, although currently government borrowing has been reduced as a result of a huge swing in household behaviour, as between 2015 and 2017 this sector changed from being net lenders of £59bn to being net borrowers of £24bn. Leaving aside exceptional trends such as this, however, the notion that reducing the government deficit by cutting expenditure or raising taxes is built on a fallacy of composition – however intuitively obvious it may seem that this must be the right way to bring government borrowing down. This is the assumption that what might make sense for an individual would be equally appropriate for the economy as a whole.

It may well be the case that individuals living beyond their means need to reduce their expenditure or to increase their incomes to bring their finances under control. If the state does this, however, its impact is not to reduce its borrowing but to tip the economy towards a recession – as austerity policies have done – because social expenditure goes up and the tax take falls, leaving the deficit substantially where it was before. The reality is that the only way to bring the government deficit under control without plunging the economy into a recession is to reduce the foreign payments deficit – something which successive governments, Labour, Coalition and Conservative, have done little or nothing to try to achieve.

If any government was nevertheless determined to reduce its deficit to zero by cutting expenditure and raising taxes whatever it took, it could succeed, but at huge cost. This is what happened in Greece over the period 2008 to 2014. Deflation took place on a sufficient scale to reduce imports to match Greek exports, eliminating the previous balance of payments deficit and thus bringing the government budget back into balance. The result, however, was to reduce Greek GDP by over a quarter in real terms.[36] This is hardly a recipe for running a successful economy in the interest of all its citizens. The UK government has had to run a large deficit because, unless we had done so, we would have suffered from the same problems as have been inflicted on Greece.

The reason why our huge balance of payments deficits have inflated the money supply as well as encouraging austerity is that the fiscal restraint which has been attempted in cutting back public expenditure has had to be offset by relaxing the money supply to stimulate private expenditure, to avoid the economy sliding backwards. This has been done by massively increasing the monetary base via Quantitative Easing, reaching a total of £435bn,[37] accompanied by rock bottom interest rates. This has made it easier for those who were already credit-worthy to borrow more. The result has been a massive increase in asset prices, which in turn has increased consumer confidence and led to consumer expenditure-based increases in demand. Consumer expenditure as a proportion of UK GDP, at 84%, is substantially higher than in almost any other country in the developed world.[38]

The risk that we now face is that the large amount of corporate and household borrowing, shown in Table 2.4, melts away as confidence falls, leaving the public sector with no alternative but massively to expand again the deficit on which it operates. This will leave the government facing another large increase in its borrowing requirement, further destabilising the country's national finances. Instead, we need to pay our way in the world, to live within our means and to pay off some of our debts instead of carrying on as we are, constantly putting off the evil day until reality catches up with us, by borrowing more and more.

Increasing disparities in life chances

The final major imbalance in the UK economy is around inequality, with three main dimensions. These are disparities in living standards and opportunities between London and the South East and the rest of the country; the gap which has opened between the achievements and prospects between millennials and those born a decade or two earlier; and between those who are wealthy and those who have not been so lucky.

All countries have inequalities and those living in democracies are usually sufficiently realistic to acknowledge that there are always going to be differences in living standards, prestige and esteem enjoyed by some people compared to others. Furthermore, it is easier to accept that some peoples' living standards are rising faster than others if almost everyone is experiencing some improvement. A much less acceptable situation is reached, as is now the case in the UK, when at least half the population have static or falling real incomes while a minority that is privileged, but not particularly deserving, is clearly doing very much better.

Reference has already been made to the huge disparity there is between the GVA generated per employee in London compared to poorer regions such as Wales and the North East. It is not just these static comparisons, however, which are so worrying. It is the direction of travel. There is no sign of the gap narrowing. On the contrary, over the past few years, the disparities have widened. It now seems hard to believe that until about the 1920s the north of England was richer than the south[39] and there was a time not so very long ago when Bradford, now one of the poorest places in the country, was among the most prosperous cities in the UK.[40]

What has happened, particularly recently, is that average living standards in London have risen in line with GDP while in poorer regions they have fallen back. Between 2007 and 2013 in the North East they fell by about 9% and in Wales by 10%, whereas in London they more or less held their own.[41] This happened because the relatively disadvantaged areas of the country simply do not have the capacity currently to pay their way in the world. This is why they depend on grants, transfers, loans and asset sales to cover the gap between what they earn and what they spend. Especially at a time and in a climate of austerity there is never enough money to reverse the remorseless underlying trends towards cut-backs to try to make the books balance.

The inter-generational inequality problem is a new one, at least on anything like the scale which is now apparent. It centres around the inability of so many young people either to obtain satisfactory employment, paying a reasonable wage or salary for a fulfilling job, or being able to buy a house or flat to provide a secure base for raising a family, thus frequently leaving them with no choice but either to stay with their parents or to rent at exorbitant cost. Some of the problem on the income side has been caused by the hollowing out of the labour market, especially in the service sector, as remuneration polarises at either end of the income spectrum. Part comes from the heavy bias there is in the education system towards academic rather than vocational training, leaving students, often weighed down with heavy debts, struggling to find reasonably paid employment which matches their qualifications. Part comes, especially outside London, from poor employment prospects generally.

The collapse of housebuilding since the 1960s[42] has generated a massive shortage of accommodation as the number of housing units expanded far more slowly than potential household formation. During the 1960s, the UK constructed an average of just over 300,000 units of accommodation a year. By the 2000s this performance had fallen to less than 150,000 per annum, with local authorities building only a derisory average of 224 units per year compared to 147,000 in the 1950s.[43] This situation has been aggravated by the major banks lending far more liberally for house purchase than for any other types of loans, driving up prices beyond the capacity of large sections of the population to pay them. In 1991, 67% of 25-34-year-olds owned their own home. Now it is 38%.[44] The result is pessimism and discontent – and distrust in the way the country is being run – among large sections of the rising generation.

Looking at the overall picture, in the UK the Gini measure of post-tax and benefit inequality rose under the Thatcher Conservative government from 0.24 in the 1970s to 0.34 by 1990. It then peaked at 0.36 under the Blair Labour government during the run-up to the 2008 crash, since when it has dropped back to hovering around 0.34. The distribution of income, has thus become slightly more even than it was in 2007, partly because the huge bonus payments paid in financial services during the run-up to the crash have fallen out of the income profile and partly because of the impact of rising minimum wages and tax changes. It is still, however, far more unequal than it was before the start of the Thatcher era and the Gini coefficient shows no signs of falling. The position on the distribution of wealth and life chances generally is even more concerning. Low interest rates and Quantitative Easing have produced an very substantial boom in the value of assets and a huge increase in wealth and life-chance inequalities as these conditions have benefitted those already well off far more than those not so fortunate. Examples of this happening are that the average value of housing in the UK as a whole rose between March 2009 and November 2017 by 46% and in London by 96.[45] Since the lowest point during the 2008 crash until January 2018, the FTSE 100 index has risen by 119%.[46] As the economy stabilised after the crash, total wealth held by the top UK decile rose between 2010 and 2014 from 25 times what was held by the bottom decile to 34 times.[47]

There are solutions to all these problems, but all of them require higher levels of investment, better job prospects, reindustrialisation and a higher rate of economic growth. There is little doubt that the regions of the UK outside London would be much more prosperous than they are at present if the proportion of UK GDP accounted by manufacturing in the regions rose sharply. This would enable them both to raise their living standards directly and to pay their way in the world, thus making them much less dependent on subventions from elsewhere. Rebalancing the UK economy towards manufacturing more generally would make our foreign payments position much more manageable and sustainable as well as producing better job prospects and creating conditions for productivity increases generally, leading to higher rates of economic growth. The millennial generation would also benefit from new job opportunities, especially if they were allied to much better and appropriate training for new employment prospects which faster growth would open up. If much higher levels of investment included a major housebuilding drive, as it should, there would be some light at the end of the tunnel for those desperate to get on the housing ladder. A huge amount in terms of developing an appealing electoral platform for social democracy therefore turns on it being possible to put forward convincing policies to get the economy to perform better.

3

The left-behind and the limits of redistribution

From its inception in 1900, supporters of the Labour Party in the UK – and indeed those who established its predecessor the Independent Labour Party (ILP), founded in 1893[1] – always entailed a somewhat uneasy alliance between those who thought they stood to gain directly from the advent of Labour administrations and those who supported Labour for rather more disinterested reasons. These shaded from idealistic support by some people for the interests of those less advantaged than themselves to others who thought that it was worth allowing for some personal financial sacrifice to achieve a less divided and more stable society than market forces, left to themselves, would produce. Similar concerns and tensions have been manifest across the western world, between those who support left-of-centre parties out of self-interest and those – the better off – with less immediate concern for their own economic interests compared to the welfare of the nation as a whole.

In the UK, as elsewhere, it was the widening of the franchise combined with rising living standards and greater prosperity which changed what might be possible. In the UK, there were significant increases in the franchise for men in 1832, 1867, 1884 and 1918, while women got the vote in 1928.[2] As industrialisation spread during the nineteenth century and education attainments and living standards rose, trades unions gained in strength. The ILP was established by trades unionists who realised that the ultimate way of gaining power and controlling resources was through government. Partly accelerated by the two world wars, within a generation these goals began to be realised. 1924 saw the election of the first Labour government, albeit with a minority of parliamentary seats in a hung parliament. There was a second Labour government in 1929, although neither lasted for long and the circumstances of the time did not allow them much scope for radical advance of Labour interests. 1945, however, saw a huge advance. The large Labour majority achieved in the July 1945 general election was built on the legacy of wartime sacrifices and national cohesion.[3]

The Labour Party which was elected in 1945 had high hopes that it was going to usher in an age of much greater equality than had been achieved so far. Clause 4 of Labour's constitution called upon the party 'To secure for the workers by hand or by brain the full fruits of their industry and the most equitable distribution thereof that may be possible upon the basis of the common ownership of the means of production distribution and exchange, and the best obtainable system of popular administration and control of each industry or service.'[4] To fulfil these aspirations, major industries covering a fifth of the economy, such as coal, the railways, steel, gas, electricity, telephones and inland transport (including road haulage) – not to mention the Bank of England – were nationalised.[5] Taxes were raised to very high levels – over 90% on the highest incomes[6] – while the welfare state, designed to cover cradle to grave, was established. These achievements were secured, however, against a background of considerable austerity, privation, rationing and controls. Astonishingly, the UK economy, whose wartime GDP had peaked in 1943 did not regain this level of output until 1953.[7] The result was that Labour achieved a much smaller parliamentary majority of only five in the 1950 general election than in 1945, and then narrowly lost the next general election in 1951 to the Conservatives, who nevertheless accepted and maintained the much larger role for the state which they inherited.[8] Whereas in the 1930s, total public expenditure had fluctuated around 20% of GDP, by the 1950s it was closer to 40%.[9]

Especially during the earlier part of the period between 1951 and 1979, it looked as though broadly speaking a settlement had been reached about how the economy was to be run which was likely to endure. This was the era of Butskellism – implying a wide area of agreement between the Conservative Rab Butler and Labour's

Hugh Gaitskell about where the balance between collectivism and free markets should lie, and how large the role of the state should be.[10] Buttressed by the success of Keynesian policies during this period, despite some set-backs, the UK economy performed reasonably well, growing at an average of 2.7% per annum between 1950 and 1975. This rate of growth, however, was below what was being achieved in the European Economic Community (EEC) during the same period, where the average was 4.5%.[11]

As the years wore on, however, the cross-party consensus began to fray. 1968 saw an upsurge in strikes in the UK, reflected in similar events in France and elsewhere. The 1970s saw an even more turbulent period as the Bretton Woods settlement collapsed and inflation combined with slower growth – stagflation – began to be an increasingly serious problem. The Keynesian consensus lacked any adequate response to the inflationary pressures, and consequently monetarism and neoliberalism took over, culminating in the election of a Conservative administration under Margaret Thatcher, with a very different agenda, in 1979.

Crucially, the period from the end of World War II until the 1970s was one where the distribution of income and wealth across the western world was relatively evenly spread. The impact of the two world wars and the destruction of wealth in the inter-war period – combined with widespread determination to aim for both fairer as well as more prosperous societies after almost half a century of war and slump – was a huge reduction in inequality from the peak reached just before the outbreak of World War I. The ratio between accumulated wealth and GDP in Germany, France and the UK all fell by about half between 1910 and 1950.[12] As a result the top percentile's share of total income, as a measure of inequality, had declined from roughly 20% to 8%, a condition which persisted until the 1970s.[13]

The result of the new monetarist and then neoliberal agenda coming to the fore was to reverse this reduction in inequality – dramatically in the case of the UK and USA and more slowly elsewhere. Over the next forty years, the proportion of total incomes going to the top 1% rose in the USA back to 18%, where it had been in the 1920s, with the UK following close behind.[14] The result was that the growth in pre-tax incomes for all but the very rich slowed up substantially in relation to the rate at which GDP was increasing – which was also slowing down. It is this double impact which has had such a devastating effect on real wage levels in the USA and UK. For large swathes of the labour force in the USA, real wages are no higher now than they were 40 years ago.[15] Wage stagnation on this scale was slower to materialise in the UK but, for many, real incomes are no higher now than they were in 2000 and for a large majority of the population, there have been no real increases in incomes at all since before the 2008 crash.[16]

Nor has the position after tax and benefits changed in any material way to offset these developments. Consistently throughout the whole period the tax and benefit system has involved significant transfers of income from roughly the top 5% of income earners to the bottom 20%, leaving all the remaining 75% roughly back where they started. Tax changes over the last forty years have, on the whole, very substantially benefitted the rich. They are still responsible for a high proportion of the total income tax take, but exemptions on capital gains and through other tax reliefs mean that the total impact on post-tax and benefit redistribution has barely changed.[17] This is why, although it is true that the post-tax and benefit distribution of income in all developed countries is considerably less unequal than pre-tax and benefits, real disposable incomes are just as stagnant as those measured gross.

In most of continental Europe and the UK, there were slow rises of disposable income during the years running up to the 2008 crash. Although performance was much less impressive than in the East, it was nevertheless sufficient to retain support for left-of-centre administrations. On the continent the advent of the euro led to speculative booms, particularly in Spain and Ireland, which raised incomes in the short term, albeit with heavy long-term costs. Policies in the UK were particularly poor in this respect. Although the UK economy grew steadily every year from when we left the Exchange Rate Mechanism (ERM) in 1992 to 2008,[18] this success was bought at a very high price in terms of the sale of UK assets to finance standards of living which were not being earned, based on an exchange rate which ensured that the UK steadily deindustrialised, making the longer-term foreign payments position progressively more precarious. It is estimated that the massive sale of UK portfolio assets during the first ten years of the present century alone generated fees and charges in the City totalling some £40bn.[19]

Looser regulation failed to contain the speculation and reckless lending which led to the 2008 crash, causing reductions in GDP, rising unemployment across the West and reduced real incomes, from which recovery has been very slow. Germany's huge trade surplus year after year made recovery in the weaker Eurozone economies exceptionally difficult to achieve. GDP did not recover its 2008 levels until 2015 in the UK, 2011 in Germany and 2017 in Spain, while Greek GDP plummeted to 25% below its previous peak.[20] Recovery in the USA has been rather faster although very large balance of payments and government deficits make sustainability look doubtful. As we draw towards the end of 2019, it looks as though growth in most western countries may be slowing down again – and with it, any realistic prospects for raising incomes for working people.

Overall, therefore, the picture across the whole of the West has been one of slowing economic growth combined with increasingly skewed distributions of income and wealth. Much of these developments have been presided over by moderate left-of-centre governments run by parties which have, as a result, steadily lost the confidence of their supporters. Where they have been in opposition, they have been unable to put forward convincing alternative policies for remedying the conditions which their electorates found increasingly intolerable. Unless social democrats can do better than this, they may never regain power again – or to be thought by their electorates to deserve to do so.

The decline in support for public ownership

One of the key dividing lines between the right and the left has been over the scale to which the state should control the economy. The right has always tended to champion a smaller state, lower taxation, privatisation, less regulation and generally to favour private enterprise over state initiatives. The left, on the other hand, has been more inclined towards intervention, more willing to see public expenditure and taxation increase, has had more confidence in public ownership and more faith in intervention and industrial strategies to improve the performance of the economy. How is social democracy likely to position itself in this debate in future?

Promoting the role of the state in the economy has always entailed a good deal of tension between those who believed that public ownership and control was a good in itself and those who thought that it should be undertaken at least primarily to improve efficiency. Going back to Karl Marx and the crusade he led to get rid of capitalism and the profit motive, there has always been a strong idealistic concern among those favouring public ownership and control that common ownership was morally better than private enterprise and that conditions along these lines were therefore the default preference.[21] The revisionist position on this issue, originally raised in Germany at the end of the nineteenth century, but still a live issue when Anthony Crosland wrote *The Future of Socialism*, published in 1956,[22] was that public ownership, and nationalisation in particular, should be judged on their practical results rather than on ideological grounds. Broadly speaking, one of the key dividing lies between the moderate and the harder left has always been opposing views on this issue, with those taking a pragmatic view generally being treated as defectors from the true faith by those with more ideological motivations.

When this divide opened up in the nineteenth century, there was only very limited practical experience on which to draw as to whether taking economic activity out of the private and into the public sphere would work – either in terms of improving the moral climate or in terms of practical outcomes. The twentieth century and beyond, however, has provided much more concrete evidence of the extent to which over-riding market forces with state ownership and control can produce better or worse outcomes. The line taken on these issues clearly has had a significant influence on the centre left's capacity to get enough of the electorate on its side, for it is now much easier to assess, in the light of experience, how these outcomes have panned out. Four reasonably firm conclusions can be drawn.

The first is that there is a very definite limit to the extent to which over-riding market signals by taking large sectors of the economy out of private hands and into state control can be successful, although in some respects the results were less clear-cut than appeared to be the case at the time. While the Soviet Union, developed on socialist lines following the 1917 revolution, had a dismal record of repression and economic hardship, its achievement in riding through the inter-war slump was much more impressive than that of most of the West. Whereas US GDP dropped by 29% between 1929 and 1932,[23] the Soviet economy grew every year during the depression in the West, bar a small drop in 1932.[24] This growth continued after World War II, getting the USA seriously worried that the USSR's GDP might soon rival that of its own.[25] During the era presided over by Leonid Brezhnev (1906-1982),[26] however, the Soviet economy became more and more stagnant until it eventually imploded in 1989,[27] leaving the world with little confidence that large-scale socialism was a desirable option. More recent experience in Venezuela and in other countries such as North Korea strongly reinforced this impression. Meanwhile China led the way as a nominally communist country with a large and flourishing private sector operated very largely on free enterprise capitalist lines.

Second, while wholesale overthrow of the private sector failed to work, it also became clear that a mixture of public and private ownership could be made to function with quite wide variations as to how much of the economy was owned by the state rather than in private hands. In some countries, such as France and Germany, the railway system is owned by the state while in others, including the UK and the USA, it is, to a significant extent, owned and operated by the private sector. The same variety of ownership is true of utilities, power companies and key industries such as steel production. Few countries now have state-owned airlines or inland freight services. Not many countries have privatised their postal service, the UK being an exception, while many countries have at least partial ownership of their car industries in public hands.[28] The general lesson learnt over the past century is that there is a wide variation in the boundaries between the public and the private sectors in mixed economies which can be made to function reasonably well. In some countries, such as France, this favourable approach is reinforced by a general tendency for the most able people to move between the private and public sectors of the economy. This does not happen to the same extent in the UK.

Third, neither private nor pubic ownership is perceived as being that satisfactory. Private-sector companies are often criticised for being greedy, short-sighted and exploitative. Those in the public sector, however, are not immune from criticism. They are often perceived to be relatively unresponsive to consumers, inclined to benefit the people running them more than their customers and to be subject to political manipulation of their pricing. For this and other reasons their record in profitability terms has often been poor, requiring substantial subsidies from the public purse. During the period in the UK when much more of the economy was nationalised than is the case now, nationalised industries such as coal, steel and aviation regularly turned in substantial losses every year, a pattern which would be much harder to tolerate nowadays[29]. A problem with publicly-owned enterprises, especially if they were making losses and thus generating no positive cash flow, was that their need for financing capital expenditure tended to push up the government's borrowing requirement in a highly unwelcome way, the result being that publicly-owned services tended to be starved of capital.

Fourth, a casualty of the ever more pragmatic approach to the benefits or disbenefits of public ownership and control, at least among most of the centre left, has been the erosion of the ideological leaning towards the notion that public ownership is morally better than having large-scale enterprises in private hands. This has happened partly because of the persuasive arguments originally advanced by Adam Smith (1723-1790)[30] that there is virtue in the market system itself in fostering behaviour from which everyone benefits and nurturing commercial society which engenders values and characteristics of its own of civic and community solidarity.[31] There has also been little evidence that public ownership acts in a redistributive way to make society as a whole more equitable.

The result of all these developments is that there is now little if any mileage among most naturally centre left voters on principle for public ownership and control, although this is not true of those further to the left. It is also important to take into account the pragmatic public support there is in the UK in 2019, for example, for renationalising the railways and capping energy prices, reflecting significant willingness among the public for more radical solutions to widely perceived problems where they think that the market is failing.[32] There are, however, large potential problems involved in financing the renationalisation of industries which currently pay significant dividends to the shareholders who now own them – often investment funds on which a wide variety of people depend for their pensions. Capping prices can also very easily slide into providing price distortions with no benefit to the country as a whole. Nor is there much – if any – evidence that changing the ownership of major industries will make the economy overall perform better, increase productivity or step up the growth rate.

Social democrats should, therefore, be wary of advocating public ownership and control as ways to increase their voter appeal. This may well have been an important part of Labour's appeal in 1945 but it is unlikely to work in the twenty-first century. The future looks like generally being a pragmatic choice about what works best, often with private ownership providing capital and market-driven efficiency but constrained by public sector regulators.

The challenge and complexity of redistribution

As already noted, one of the criticisms of industries in public ownership, and thus at least partly protected from the financial pressures with which private companies have to contend, is the tendency for their employees to use this advantage to benefit themselves rather than their customers or the public at large. There has always been a similar problem for public expenditure generally, which is the tendency for those who are well off to benefit disproportionately from it.

To some extent, this is inevitable. Those with larger incomes tend to consume more of almost everything than those who are poorer, and publicly provided services are no exception. This makes using the powers of the state to redistribute income successfully surprisingly difficult. The net result is that there is a significant transfer of real incomes through the tax and benefit system from roughly the top 5% of income earners to the bottom 20% while all the remaining 75% finish up broadly speaking back where they started. There are a number of different reasons why this is the case.

The tax and benefit system is not just designed to achieve redistribution but to achieve many other objectives as well. Quite a number conflict with a simply redistributive agenda. This is particularly the case, for example, with 'sin taxes' on cigarettes, alcohol and sugary foods, all of which tend to account for a higher proportion of the spending of poorer rather than richer people, but other heads of both taxation and expenditure have the same impact. Expenditure on the arts tends disproportionately to benefit relatively high earners, as do subsidies to most forms of public transport. Aviation is clearly used more by those who are better off and is both barely taxed and heavily subsidised. Tax breaks often have the same effect, such as the Entrepreneur's Allowance, designed to encourage business enterprise, which allowed capital gains to be taxed at only 10%, thus notoriously enabling very high earning hedge fund managers to pay lower effective rates of tax on their earnings than the cleaners in their offices, who were earning a small fraction of their employers' remuneration.

Continual efforts to tweak the tax and benefit system supposedly to iron out anomalies have often made the problems worse by making them more complicated and sometimes supposed attempts at rationalisation and simplification such as Universal Credit have finished up by being so difficult to implement that, at least in the short term, they have made redistribution less rather than more effective. Especially in these circumstances, there is also a danger then that the cost of tax collection and its disbursement becomes disproportionately high.

The huge disparities in the gross value added (GVA) per employee between London and other regions of the UK pre-empt a substantial proportion of the tax and benefit system. As we have seen, the average GVA per employee in London in 2017 was £49k whereas in Wales and the North East it was about £20k.[33] The primary reason for this state of affairs is deindustrialisation, which means that about three quarters of the UK consists of towns, cities and country areas which do not have enough to sell to the rest of the world to pay for the standards of living enjoyed by their citizens.

The shortfall of revenue in many parts of the country, flowing from the lack of production of enough goods and services which the rest of the world wants to buy, leaves a large gap in post-tax and benefit incomes between London and the rest of the country. This has to be made up by benefits, grants, loans and subsidies, very largely taking place within the public sector. This is why the very heavy cuts recently in local government expenditure have had a significant effect in increasing regional inequality. Overall, however, the effect of transfers to deal with regional inequalities has been to pre-empt a substantial proportion of redistributive expenditure, which might have been concentrated on reducing the post-tax dispersion of incomes between socio-economic groups, to trying to cope with regional imbalances.

Redistribution through the tax and benefit system is not helped by a large accretion of measures which may have made some sort of political sense when they were introduced but which now look extremely difficult to justify. Should we really provide free travel to all pensioners now that those over pension age are, as a whole, better off than those in work?[34] Does it really make sense to pay everyone, irrespective of their means, a £200 tax-free heating allowance every year? The problem with benefits such as these is that, once people have got used to receiving them, removing them becomes unpopular and difficult. It is a well-known phenomenon, which applies to the tax and benefit system as much as to anything else, that people are much more upset by losing something to which they are accustomed than they are to forgoing something new which they have not had before. Unfortunately, however, this makes it much more difficult than might otherwise be the case to avoid the tax system accumulating anomalies which are very difficult to get rid of but which pre-empt more sensible use of the limited redistributive capacity available.

Allied to this is the chronic tendency for at least some benefits, once introduced, to grow in size. Perhaps the most conspicuous examples are the subsidies to housing costs and the top-up arrangements for those on low wages. In both these cases, the availability of subsidies helps to create circumstances which justify the sums involved increasing. Housing subsidies increase the demand for housing, raising its cost and thus causing the demand for housing subsidies to go up. Topping up low wages has a similar effect, particularly if the level at which income tax starts being levied is raised but national insurance payments remain in place as they are now. Larger and larger top-ups are needed to close the widening gap between real earnings and the cost of living.

It is striking to see how powerful these pressures have been. In the 1970s, revenue housing subsidies represented only about a third of government funded support for housing, with the balance going on capital expenditure. Now, about two thirds of the total goes to revenue and one third to capital expenditure, as revenue support costs rose from £16.6bn in 1995/96 to £24.1bn in 2015/16.[35] Similarly, top-ups for low wages costs had reached £11bn a year by the mid-2010s.[36] In both these cases there is a measure of redistribution to make the post-tax and benefit position fairer than it might have been without them, but at the cost of making the pre-tax distribution more uneven than might otherwise have been the case.

Perhaps the most important of all the reasons why using the tax and benefit system to redistribute incomes from rich to poor has turned out to be so difficult has been the ability of members of the middle class to manipulate the system to their advantage. Some of this process is overt, such as buying or renting housing near to the best public sector schools. Much of it, however, is more difficult to identify, stemming partly from the fact that richer people tend to use all sorts of resources more intensively than those who are poorer. The better-off then tend to benefit disproportionately from public expenditure on roads, rail, public facilities and even hospitals if they are more effective, as they often are, at claiming use of the facilities and services available. It is also mostly middle-class people who, as civil servants, local authority officers and NHS administrators, run the public sector of the economy and who feel entitled to be paid well and to have generous inflation-proofed pensions which the private sector can no longer afford.

All these considerations explain why public expenditure,

however it may be justified by its merits and benefits to the public at large, is not disproportionately of advantage to large numbers of people on or below average incomes. This is the part of the electorate with incomes stretching from between roughly 20% to 50% on the income scale, i.e. from those who have 20% of the population with incomes smaller than theirs to those with 50% whose incomes which are greater. They are largely the same people who have traditionally been Labour's bedrock working-class supporters.

Like all parties in government, social democrats have to claim to be able run the tax system, the public sector and indeed the economy generally more efficiently than the opposition. Whether this can realistically include a significant redistributive agenda, however, is likely to be particularly problematic if as large a proportion of the tax and benefit system is pre-empted by transfers particularly to deal with regional imbalances – as is evidently the case in the UK at present. This means that one of the key reasons for voting for left rather than right-of-centre parties – on redistributive grounds – has currently been largely eroded. There may well be scope for winning back some ground, if there were fewer disparities in pre-tax and benefit income levels between all the regions of country, easing the position, for example, on some of the austerity measures which have hit disadvantaged sections of the population hardest. If the centre left is going to win back the support it needs, however, it may have to concentrate on appealing to the electorate not so much on redistributive grounds but as being both more effective in government at promoting economic growth than the right. It will also need to be more empathetic. This is a new challenge.

Taking back control?

Are there other ways of redistributing not just material resources but additional key elements in life, such as power and influence, status and self-esteem? It is clear from all the polling which was done at the time of the 2016 EU referendum that by far the most important reason why so many people among the electorate voted for Leave rather than Remain was a feeling of powerlessness, which clearly many people thought that voting Leave might assuage. Is there a left-of-centre message which can be delivered in response?

Perhaps we should start by asking why did so many people feel so powerless. Here are some answers.

Even a cursory glance at the results of the 2016 EU referendum shows that there is a high correlation, particularly in England, between the areas of the UK which have clearly done well out of globalisation and those which have, on the whole, suffered from it. London voted strongly for Remain while Wales, the Midlands and the North of England mainly had Leave majorities. It is not difficult to see why this happened. London has done exceptionally well recently. It has become one of the wealthiest areas in the EU[37] as a result of its commercial success internationally, particularly in financial services, and because of its cultural pre-eminence and world class ambience, buttressed by its universities and its central role in the UK economy in politics and economics and almost all other respects.

Most of the rest of the country, however, has done nothing like as well, partly because London's achievements have been secured on the back of policies which have generally had adverse ramifications on the rest of the county. The liberal trading environment which reinforced London's pre-eminence has led to deindustrialisation in much of the rest of the country as trading conditions which favoured London have had the opposite effect in the provinces. The consequent decline in many parts of the country in their capacity to support themselves has led to large areas being heavily dependent on transfers from London but still facing stagnant or falling living standards while public services have been cut back. Understandably, having large areas of the country unable to support themselves economically, and thus dependent on the somewhat grudging largesse of London, has left both local government and their electorates feeling powerless and unappreciated.

The huge gap in gross value added per employee per year – £49k in London in 2017 compared to £20k in the North East in Wales[38] – is inevitably a reflection of the quality of jobs on offer. Relatively high value-added jobs in manufacturing – and mining – have given way to service sector jobs in sectors such as retailing and tourism, where productivity is low and difficult to increase. There is also evidence that there is considerably less job satisfaction and status attached to these sorts of jobs than to those which they replaced. This has been a particularly difficult transition for men used to being the breadwinners, who now find themselves competing with women at least as capable of doing most service sector jobs as they are.

Part of this, in turn, is a reflection of the many ways in which the job market is changing as digitalisation becomes everywhere more prevalent, producing wide-ranging uncertainty about which jobs are still going to be there at all in a few years' time. Unemployment may be at record low levels – although partly offset by increased part-time working[39] – but job security has gone down not only in the gig economy but also more widely as the economy adapts to machine learning and artificial intelligence. There is plenty of evidence that developments along these lines tend to favour those who are well educated and trained at the expense of those without these qualifications, increasing the uncertainty over the prospects for millions of people who feel – with considerable justification – that they face an uncertain future which is unlikely to produce a better outcome than they have achieved so far and which may well lead to an even more difficult and challenging future.

Trade union solidarity has always been a powerful source of working-class control over the environment in which work took place, but trade union membership has declined steeply. Total UK membership peaked at 13.2m in 1979 but had more than halved by the mid-2010s to 6.2m.[40] This happened over a period when both the population and the total workforce have significantly increased, making the decline in trade union membership in relation to potential membership even more marked. Trade union membership is also now much more heavily concentrated in the public sector than used to be the case and considerably more orientated to white collar work than to manual labour. In the private sector, trade union membership was always easier to manage in large industrial undertakings than in more fragmented service sector companies so the decline in membership, especially outside the public sector, is heavily correlated with the decline in manufacturing.

Over the last forty years, and particularly during the Thatcher government period, the legal status of trade unions was substantially weakened, with the role of trade unions in protecting the interests of worker being provided instead – at least in part – by government regulation on health and safety, paternity rights, minimum wages, etc. There may have been a problem with over-mighty unions during the years running up to the 1980s, but the effect of clipping their wings in the way in which this was done left large swathes of the country's labour force with considerably less control over their working environments than they had before. No doubt, this has partly been why unemployment in the UK has fallen so low without causing any significant inflationary pressures and why it has been relatively easy to change working methods and to get rid of the restrictive practices which had given some trade unions a bad name during the post-war years. The single union agreements negotiated in the car industry were particularly good examples of how modern trade unionism can work well. We should not lose sight, however, of the fact that the decline of trade unions has greatly increased the power and control of management and company owners at the expense of their employees.

The UK is a an exceptionally centralised state with London in a pre-eminent position in almost all respects. London is not only much richer than the rest of the country; it is also in a key position from a cultural and political perspective. This phenomenon has led to a variety of proposals to try to redress the balance, including the Northern Powerhouse and the equivalent Midlands Engine. It has driven attempts to redress the regional balance such as the HS2 project. It successfully got substantial sections of the BBC's activities moved to Salford and it has been behind proposals to move the Bank of England to Birmingham.

The pressing need to refurbish the Palace of Westminster followed by the decision to move Parliament – at a cost of some £1.5bn[41] – to another location in London instead of outside the capital shows how difficult it is to change the balance between London and the regions. The real problem is that political power springs from economic heft and London is not only much stronger economically than the rest of the country but continues to steadily pull ahead. There is little sign of this tendency being reversed. As long as these trends persist it is difficult to see how any feasible changes in institutions and the way that political power is diffused at least through England will change. Scotland may be a different matter, although it may well be that the Barnett formula, which has the effect of transferring some £1,720[42] per head of the Scottish population per year from London to Scotland is the clinching reason why the Scottish Nationalist Party has so far failed to muster a convincing, stable majority in favour of independence. But support for the SNP partly reflects resentment at the dominant role of London, which is a sentiment widely shared among the English regions.

Conclusion

In the end, however, it is surely the huge regional disparities there are in economic performance between London and the regions which determines why so many people in Wales, the Midlands and the North of England felt so disempowered that in protest they voted to leave the European Union in the 2016 EU referendum. As we have seen, the most important reason why they did this was because doing so reflected their general sense that they lived in an environment where control of their lives and their futures had been weaned away from them. Some of this was due to economic circumstances but much of it was not directly related to these at all. One of the more striking poll results at the time of the EU referendum was that six in ten of those who voted for Leave were quite prepared to accept that doing so might lead to a worsening in their financial circumstances. In their opinion – rightly or wrongly – being out of the control of the EU was sufficiently important to them for them to be willing to have a lower standard of living to achieve this objective.[43]

Power and economic success, however, are inextricably linked and there cannot be much doubt about the fact that the way to make most people outside London feel more content with their lot is to get the regions of the UK outside London performing better. The towns and cities outside London have to have more to sell to the rest of the world, in the UK and abroad – indeed ideally enough to enable them fully to pay their way as they used to be able to do until about a century ago. The only way in which this condition is going to be able to be fulfilled is to restore to them a reasonable degree of manufacturing, all of which takes us back to the arguments in earlier chapters of this book. The key to rebalancing the UK economy and to dealing with regional imbalances as well as many other negative features of the current UK economy – and factors such as self-respect as well – is to deal with the imbalances which plague our economy. We need to make sure that we invest as much as other countries do, that we manufacture enough of what the world wants to buy for the whole country to be able to pay its way, that our exports are competitive enough to pay for all our imports, that we no longer have to borrow or to sell assets to sustain our living standards and that we try to put some cap on inequality.

4

Coming apart: the cleavages opening up within society

Social democratic parties have only been able to win elections as successfully as they have done by combining together the voting power of their working- and middle-class supporters. Their current failure to muster sufficient support is not primarily caused by defections among those who are better off. It is the erosion of their working-class vote which has been, and is, the problem.[1] There is no single reason why this has happened. It has been the consequence of a variety of factors coming together to cause a substantial rupture in feelings of identity and empathy from which it may well be difficult for social democratic parties to recover.

As we have seen in previous chapters, some of this alienation has been caused both by the centre left's poor economic growth record and its redistributive agenda not working effectively. The problem, however, is not just stagnant incomes and the failure of taxation and spending to make many working-class people better off. A significant number of other changes and developments have had decisive impacts on the way in which many working-class people view the middle-class, whose party allegiance most of them used to share, and this chapter considers what they might be. It looks first at the underlying factors which have generated the gaps in empathy which are now apparent, examines their resulting impacts, considers the overt symptoms which have materialised and then evaluates their political implications on the probable future of social democracy.

Underlying causes of divisions

Education

In 1950, only 17,300 students were awarded first degrees at UK universities while 2,400 were awarded higher degrees. By 2010, the corresponding figures were 331,000 and 182,600. In 1950, 30% of 15-year-olds and 7% of 17-year-olds were being educated on a full-time basis in England and Wales. By 2010, 88% of 16-year-olds and 76% of 17-year-olds were in full-time education.[2] These changes were the result of the huge expansion in education, especially at tertiary level, which took place during the decades following the end of World War II. This meant that large numbers of working-class people who, on the basis of their innate ability, could easily have qualified for university places, left school at 15 during the early years after World War II, often going into manual jobs. This provided a large cadre of very able working-class leaders who, through trade union activity and in other ways, fought their way to the top. In Clement Attlee's 1945 cabinet at least a third of its members had working class backgrounds, including towering figures such as Ernest Bevin, Herbert Morrison and Aneurin Bevan.[3]

Now, the situation is very different. There are almost no working-class Labour Members of Parliament and none in the shadow cabinet. Only 3% of MPs elected in 2017 had had blue-collar jobs before being elected, while 87% of all MPs now have degrees – 24% from Oxford or Cambridge, although the current shadow cabinet contains mostly alumni from red brick universities.[4] Our education system has been very effective at providing a ladder for exceptionally able working-class people, propelling them into middle-class occupations, lifestyles and attitudes. The effect, however, has been to make the pool of talent on which social democratic political leadership draws increasingly unrepresentative of the points of view and values of the working-class voters on which success at the polls heavily depends. This inevitably makes it much more difficult for these traditional Labour voters to empathise with predominately middle-class centre left political leaders with whom they have less and less in common.

Globalisation

For nearly all the period after World War II, international trade grew much more rapidly than world GDP. Between 1980 and 2002 world trade trebled while world output doubled.[5] If, as is argued in the earlier sections of this book, the UK and other countries in the West had made sure that their economic policies maintained their competitiveness with the rising economic powers in the East, increasing trade intercourse could have been to the roughly equal benefit of all sections of the labour force. This is not, however, what happened – and by a very wide margin.

The reason is that the neoliberal disregard for manufacturing during recent decades while the West's currencies got stronger and stronger in relation to those in the East, did not make much difference to the international competitiveness of either the UK's services sector or its high-tech manufacturing, both of which are relatively price insensitive. It did, however, have a massive negative impact on medium- and low-tech manufacturing, where price is crucial. As a result, metropolitan areas, particularly London, flourished as high-paying service sector jobs proliferated, not least in financial services, while industry languished in much of the rest of the country. Incomes and lifestyles among the globalised, metropolitan elite soared up while cut-backs and factory closures stunted the job prospects of millions of people previously employed in industrial jobs. Between the 1970s and now the number of people working in manufacturing fell by almost 60% while the number in services rose by just over 70%. Over the same period the number of miners tumbled from 328k to 62k.[6] Of course, working underground was always a tough, dangerous occupation but it was a relatively well-paid job, and one which carried a great deal of respect with it, for which stacking shelves in a supermarket was no substitute.

Deindustrialisation

As late as 1970, just under a third of UK GDP came from manufacturing. Now the ratio is less than 10%.[7] The losers have included large numbers of skilled and semi-skilled people who have been left with no adequate future opportunities to use the knowledge and experience they had accumulated in their previous industrial jobs. In some areas of the country, particularly in the South East new job opportunities were created fast enough to replace those which had been lost but in many parts of the country this did not happen. As a result, the job opportunities which were available, particularly for older men, tended to be more insecure and lower paid. This is why there was such a sharp widening of the gross value added per employee in the metropolitan areas of the UK, particularly London, and the regions. Whereas London had more or less held its own in average real wage terms since the 2008 crash, in Wales real wages fell by 10% and by in the North East by 9%.[8]

The impact that deindustrialisation has had on job prospects is highlighted by the fact that jobs in manufacturing generate wages which are nearly 20% higher than the average for the economy as a whole.[9] While there is no gainsaying that globalisation has been of massive benefit to millions of people who have been lifted out of poverty by the economic growth which it has helped to foster, it is also clear that these benefits have not been equally shared, particularly by blue collar workers across nearly all of the West. In the USA, hourly remuneration for blue-collar workers has never recovered from the peak it reached in the 1980s,[10] over 30 years ago, fuelling the campaign which got President Trump elected, while similar responses are visible in France and many other European countries. The results of the 2016 EU referendum in the UK by constituency largely reflect the divisions between those areas of the country which had generally benefitted from globalisation and those which had not done so.

Immigration

Another important dividing factor between middle-class and working-class people in recent years has been their respective experiences of and attitudes to immigration, particularly on the scale which materialised in the mid-2100s, when it peaked. Figure 4.1 provides the net figures.

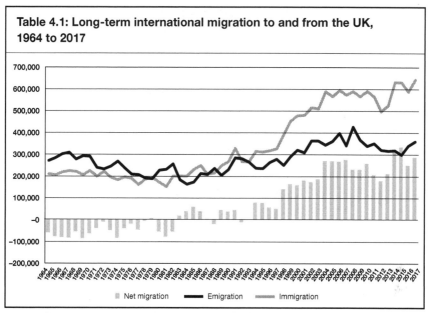

Table 4.1: Long-term international migration to and from the UK, 1964 to 2017

Source: Office for National Statistics long-term international migration data.

Generally speaking, the view taken by the successful metropolitan elite was to welcome large-scale immigration. Many thought that immigration was a good thing *per se* and that open borders built internationalism, which they strongly supported. Others welcomed the arrival of large numbers of young, ambitious people with strong work ethics, only too pleased to work for relatively low wages as waiters, gardeners and *au pairs*, from which they personally benefitted, or to be willing to do a wide variety of jobs which indigenous UK citizens seemed unwilling to take on. At a time when employment was almost full, companies and organisations like the National Health Service were only too happy to fill vacancies by recruiting among immigrants. These positive views on immigration were evidently shared by the then Labour government which decided to allow unrestricted immigration to the UK without delay from the Accession countries which joined the EU in 2004, although the UK was under no EU obligation to do so.[11] The numbers involved were then hugely underestimated. Instead of the low tens of thousands of net immigrants from Poland who were expected, by 2016 the Polish population in the UK had grown to 91,000.

By the same time, the number of Romanians and Bulgarians together had risen to 413k.[12]

The view taken on immigration, especially on this scale, among most working-class communities, however, was very different. Most were reasonably tolerant of individual immigrants but thought that the numbers allowed to enter the country, especially if they were not highly skilled, were much too large. Some of their concern was cultural – the impact of rapid changes on traditional lifestyles. Much of it was economic – the threat of wages being held down by competition from people with considerably lower wage expectations than those held by UK citizens, and the pressure on social facilities such as schools and hospitals. Although it was rightly argued that immigrants provided services as well as using them, there was ample evidence that much too little was being invested in social facilities in capital terms to keep up with the rate at which the population was rising. In summary, a large proportion of working people not only had a very different view of immigration from most social democratic leaders, but strongly resented the fact that that these views were often despised as being racist and bigoted. Sometimes they may have been but most of the time they reflected genuine concerns about the availability of educational and medical services, or job competition from people with low wage expectations, which centre left politicians ignored at their peril.

AI and changing work patterns

Another factor which has had a sizeable impact on relationships between skilled and semi-skilled working people and the political elite has been changes in working patterns even though they are mostly not under the control of the government but are of universal significance. These are particularly concerned with the radical changes in the nature of work which have been and still are taking place, including all the implications of artificial intelligence and machine learning.

Over recent decades, there have been a number of developments which have had a tendency to make it more difficult for working class people, especially men, to maintain the ratios between their remuneration and that of those higher up the income scales. The switch in the UK's economy from manufacturing to services has made it much more problematic for trades unions to maintain the differentials which used to exist. A much larger proportion of the labour force now consists of women than used to be the case, with inevitable downgrading of the primacy of the male bread-winner. As technology and mechanisation have developed, physical strength has become less important in relation to mental dexterity, a factor which the advance of artificial intelligence and machine learning can only increase. Work has become more insecure, with an increasing proportion of those in work not being employed full-time and therefore covered by employment protection legislation.

All of these trends have made life more difficult for those affected by them, especially for older men in the relatively poor regions of the country. Inevitably, those experiencing not only relative but also absolute decline in their living standards and life opportunities feel resentful, especially if they don't believe that the people they elect to look after their interests really understand the impact that these changes are having on them or respect the problems they face.

Communications

Finally, there is the role of social media and all the other means of communication there are which nowadays shape the way the community thinks of itself. There are nearly 33m active Facebook users in the UK.[13] Clearly some are more prone to be influenced than others, but it is generally recognised that the impact of social media generally has been very significant – especially as a result of carefully targeted messaging – and inclined to reinforce divisive views by acting as a sound box and amplifier for whatever views any participant may have had to start with. In the meantime radio, television and the press are largely run by people who are members of the metropolitan elite whose views are then inevitably reflected in the content of the media they control. It is hardly surprising that there are allegations of bias and group-think when half of the UK's leading columnists have been educated at public school, and more than half are graduates from Oxford or Cambridge universities. Only one in ten are from working class backgrounds.[14]

Of course a section of the press – newspapers such as *The Sun* and *The Mirror* – are orientated towards working-class readers, as are many television programmes, and a variety of political opinions are available from which readers can choose. The overall tone, however, is inevitably set by those responsible for creating the content which is disseminated. It is hard to believe that the gulf between the lifestyles, attitudes and values of those who control the media and those who are on the receiving end has nothing to do with the corresponding lack of understanding there is between them.

The consequences for social democratic values

The previous section described what appear to be the main causes of the rise of discontent, generating the rise in national populism which has taken place. This section reviews how these have played out, highlighting the extent to which they are likely to threaten support for social democratic attitudes and values.

Attitudes to the EU and internationalism

A key area relates to international organisations and, in particular, the European Union. To a large extent, centre left leaders across Europe have tended to regard the evolution of the EU as a benign development. They welcomed the international co-operation which closer working together entailed and enthusiastically supported the EU's role in bringing together all the countries involved in closer political union. They welcomed the advent of Spain and Greece to the Union in the 1980s and the East European Accession states in the 2000s, as all these countries became democracies.[15] They acquiesced without much demur in the curtailments of national sovereignty which flowed from the succession of treaties – Maastricht, Amsterdam, Nice and Lisbon[16] – which consolidated the increasingly dominant role of the EU institutions, particularly the Commission and the European Parliament. They supported the moves towards monetary union initiated by Jaques Delors in the 1990s, after the demise of the Exchange Rate Mechanism, and welcomed the establishment of the Eurozone.[17]

This positive attitude to the development of the EU's role and further integration has not, however, been shared by large sections of the population across Europe. Instead there has been resentment at the control which overtly supra-national bodies have exercised over the policies pursued by the countries making up the EU, particularly around emotive issues such as migration. These negative views have been exacerbated by high levels of unemployment and low growth rates across most of the EU, for which the establishment of the euro is widely perceived as being to blame. Italy has had no increase in GDP per head since 2000.[18] The treatment meted out to Portugal, Ireland and particularly Greece, when they needed bail-outs following the 2008 crash, stiffened resistance to EU hegemony. Portuguese GDP per head in 2016 was almost the same as it had been in 2007 while the drop in Greece was 25%.[19]

The reality is that for most people – particularly those not particularly attracted to globalisation – their loyalty focus is very much on the nation state to which they belong rather than to international institutions. Relatively uncritical support for the EU by the vast majority of social democratic leaders has not therefore chimed well with the perceptions of large numbers of their potential supporters.

Identity

Historically, the main drivers of social democracy have been to do with economics and power. Its main concern has been improving the living standards particularly of working people and giving them more control over their environment, their jobs and their future. Recently, however, there has been a noticeable shift of emphasis away from these goals and towards non-economic issues around identity, particularly to do with race, gender and sexuality.

These developments have been partly a reflection of changes in attitudes which have taken place across the political spectrum and which, while not universally accepted, are very largely common ground everywhere. Overtly racist attitudes, although not totally eliminated, are now very widely regarded as unacceptable. The degree of racial integration in cities like London, compared to the situation only a generation ago, is remarkable. The 2011 census showed 36.7% of London's residents were born abroad – with 24.5%

coming from outside Europe.[20] There is still a significant pay gap between men and women – 18.4% in the UK 2018[21] – but the role and status of women in the labour force is much higher than it was and looks as though it will continue climbing. 54% of all training level doctors in 2011[22] were female, and more than half of those starting out as barristers nowadays are too.[23] Both professions until recently were very largely male preserves. Homosexuality and same-sex marriages are an accepted part of the social fabric. Issues around gender identification are still nearer the frontier of what is mainstream but are very much on the agenda.

These are issues, however, on which there may be large majorities who take a tolerant view, but there are still significant minorities who take a different stance. The rapid change in social attitudes which has taken place has left a gap between most of the population and a section of it which feels much more comfortable with traditional attitudes than with the new ones to which most of the population adhere. This is yet another area in which national populism can find fertile ground

Lifestyles

Widening disparities in incomes and life-chances generally have inevitably led to diverging lifestyles and expectations. Among most of the metropolitan elite, their standards of living are high enough for them to be a long way away from the breadline. With relatively secure and well-paid jobs, they can look forward to the future with considerable confidence. Those not already established on the housing ladder may find accommodation a struggle but generally a rich and arid varied cultural and material lifestyle is readily available, with slowly rising real incomes being a realistic and attractive prospect. Children brought up in this environment start off with advantages of confidence, education, training and skills which young people in less advantaged environments all too often lack

For many people outside this favoured circle, the prospects are much bleaker. With static or falling real incomes, crumbing local services, life is often much more of struggle. A generation brought up to expect that rising prosperity would always provide a comforting hinterland, a downgrading of expectations to one where most people expect their children to be no better off – and quite possibly worse off – than they are, is a wrenching and dispiriting change. With limited job prospects owing to the precarious economic position of many of the areas of the country outside the South-East and a few university towns, the future looks much more insecure and problematic.

Empathy and respect

A baleful consequence of these widening divisions is an increasingly prevalent feeling among those who have been disadvantaged by all the developments described above that they are not really respected by their better-off fellow citizens, who have little empathy for their values, attitudes, and concerns. This very much came to the surface over Brexit. Many Remainers simply could not understand why so many people had voted Leave. Convinced that they were right, Remainers were very much inclined to regard people who voted Leave as being old, white, under-educated stupid and racist. They believed that if only the advantages of the UK continuing to be a member of the EU were properly explained to Leavers they would understand why they ought to have voted Remain and would the vote to stay in the EU, if given the opportunity to do so.

Whatever the relative merits of Remain or Leave, this was regarded as an extraordinarily patronising attitude by most Leave voters, whose reasons for voting Leave were well articulated. Of the motives for voting Leave, polling by Lord Ashcroft showed that the strongest motivating factor – accounting for almost 50% – was to do with democracy and control while a third was related to concerns over immigration.[24] This is why six out of ten Leavers thought a worse economic outlook a price worth paying and four out of ten thought that a relative losing his or her job was worth it too.[25] Metropolitan Remain voters may disagree with the outcome of the 2016 EU referendum but this is a different matter from saying that those who voted Leave did not understand what they were voting for. By their lights, they plainly did – at least as much as was the case with those who voted Remain. Remainers' inability to appreciate why so many Leave voters voted the way they did, and their inclination to disparage their reasons for doing so, however, has been deeply damaging.

Distrust

Perhaps the key over-riding consequence of the trends which have manifested themselves over recent decades has been the erosion of trust between large sections of the population and the political elite whose function it has been to try to represent them.

Undoubtedly Brexit has been substantially to blame. Extravagant claims by both sides did not help. The £350m a week that the Leave side claimed would be available for the NHS, and the grossly pessimistic economic forecasts produced by Remainers, did nothing to add positively to anyone's reputation. Nor has the way the Brexit negotiations with the EU, which have been thought by most of the population to have been badly mishandled, added to the lustre of the government. Nor indeed has the spectacle of the House of Commons being unable to come to any consensus on the way ahead with Brexit contributed positively to its reputation. Over 80% of the MPs elected in 2017 for either the Labour or Conservative parties did so on manifestos promising to implement the outcome of the 2016 EU referendum. It is hard, however, to avoid the impression that a majority of the 75% to 80% Remain majority in the House of Commons has been doing its best to water down or to reverse this commitment.

It is not just Brexit, however, which has been responsible for this breakdown in trust. The events around Brexit have acted as a trigger rather than a fundamental cause of the trends which have materialised, which in closely related ways are mirrored right cross the western world.

The impact on our politics

Axis changes

Ever since the British parliamentary system began to evolve, there has been a split on broadly ideological lines between the two main contending parties. On the left initially were the Whigs and then the Liberal Party, supplanted in the early twentieth century by the Labour Party, while on the right were the Conservatives. The fundamental difference between these parties was that those on the left were more committed to income, wealth and life chance redistribution and a rather larger and more intrusive role for the state.

Increasingly recently, however, the spectrum on which voting intentions are spread has shifted away from being along the traditional left/right lines to being orientated along what might be called a nativist/globaliser axis. The key characteristics on each side of this split will by now be familiar. Nativists tend to be culturally conservative and economically pragmatic while globalisers are culturally and economically more liberal and some of them at least, more driven by economic ideology. Whereas both Labour and Conservatives have with varying degrees of enthusiasm had ideologically driven economic agendas – shrinking the role of the state in the case of the Conservatives and increasing it, especially recently, in the case of Labour – nativists tend to take a more instrumental approach. They are not against nationalisation if, for example, their perception is that trying to run the railway system with track separated from rolling stock does not work, but they are not particularly in favour or against public ownership on principle. Similarly, although they are no keener than anyone else on unnecessary regulation or very high levels of personal taxation on people with relatively low incomes, they are not driven by a principled drive to make the role of the state smaller. On the contrary, they tend to be strong supporters of the welfare state.

Recently, perhaps the most conspicuous dividing line between the two camps has been their attitude to Brexit. Nativists are much more likely to be in the Leave rather than the Remain camp, with the opposite true of globalisers. This is because, both from a cultural and an economic standpoint, support for Brexit chimes in much more strongly with the attitudes, beliefs and aspirations of nativist Leavers than it does to globalised Remainers – and vice versa. The key divide is not therefore along left/right ideological lines. It is between different cultural and economic visions of how the country should be run.

On the continent, where proportional voting is much more common than it is in the UK, political parties orientated to capturing the support of their varying versions of nativism have already established substantial electoral footholds. Some of these parties, such as the National Rally (which used to be called the National Front) in France, are on the right while others such as Syriza in Greece are much more left orientated. Fidesz in Hungary is already the government party, as is The Law and Justice Party in Poland.[26] In the UK, with its first-past-the-post system, it is much more difficult for rising parties to cut through the electoral barriers to getting significant numbers of MPs elected. This is why in the UK we have almost no MPs who represent nativist views. This situation, however, may well not continue.

Voting volatility

Since World War I, there has been a tendency for the proportion of votes cast in general elections the for either Labour or Conservative Parties to decline, although 2017 was an exception. In 1951, 97% of the votes cast were for either the Labour or Conservative Parties whereas in 2015, this had dropped to 67%. In 2017, however, over 80% of all MPs were elected on either Labour or Conservative manifestos. Both of the then main parties promised to implement the 2016 EU referendum outcome on Brexit. These promises squeezed the UKIP vote down to 1.8%.[27]

Since then, especially in the light of the inconclusive Brexit negotiations and the consequent unpopularity of the Conservative government, combined with ever increasing distrust in our governing class generally, the position has become much more volatile. Successive polls have showed increasing proportions of the electorate indicating that neither of the major political parties represented their interests and merited their support. It has become increasingly apparent that the attitudes and values espoused by both the Labour and Conservative Parties are out of synch with those of large sections of the voting population. The crucial question is where this is likely to lead.

At the moment, there is not yet an avowedly nativist party although the Brexit Party clearly fills some of that role now that

UKIP has imploded. Support for the Brexit Party, however, clearly depends heavily on Brexit remaining a hotly contentious issue and this may not be the way in which events pan out. If the Conservatives succeed in concluding a reasonably satisfactory exit from the EU, the Brexit Party, having lost the main reason for is existence, may well lose much of its support, allowing Brexit Party voters to be attracted back very probably mainly to the Conservatives. Whether the Brexit Party, perhaps under another name, would then be able to put forward a sufficiently well thought through, comprehensive and attractive programme to attract sufficient numbers of votes to win elections – without Brexit as a major reason for the electorate supporting it – remains to be seen. If Brexit continues to be a highly contentious and divisive issue, however, then the Brexit Party could continue to flourish.

Support for the Labour Party has been leached away both by Remainers defecting to the Lib Dems and Leavers switching to the Brexit Party, as Labour's policy of studied ambiguity on whether to support a second referendum and to commit the Party to being fully committed to Remain did not succeed in holding support together. As long as Brexit remains as salient an issue as it is at the moment, Labour seems unlikely to make a significant recovery. If Brexit becomes less significant, Labour's fortunes may revive – although whether the country is ready to vote *en masse* for a party with as far left an agenda as Labour is currently promising remains to be tested. The Lib Dems may continue to hold their own.

Overall, it seems more likely that Brexit will rumble on for some years as a live issue, and that, as a result, none of our major political parties may be able to secure the 40% plus of the votes cast in a general election to enable it to form a majority government. It seems more likely that the outcome for some time will be that some combination of each of the four national parties – Conservative, Brexit, Labour and the Lib Dems, all with the support of somewhere between a fifth and a third of the electorate – will be forced to form coalition administrations. The big issue for social democracy in these circumstances is whether it will be able to attract back a sufficiently large percentage of the electorate to become again the force that it until relatively recently used to be.

Policy platforms

All political parties have to allow for some measure of disagreement among their members and supporters. The ideological differences between the Labour and Conservative parties on redistribution and the size and role of the state have provided something of a framework in which these differences can exist. A major problem for the nationalist populist parties which have emerged across the West is that they have lacked this kind of constraint, which has made it difficult for them to agree clear platforms with sufficient appeal and coherence to appeal to a wide enough section of the electorate to enable them to form governments. In recent years, however, this situation has started to change, as can be seen in countries such as Greece, Italy, Hungary and Poland, where national populists are or have been in control.

The problem faced by these sorts of parties is to develop sufficiently coherent policies to attract enough of the non-nativist components of the electorate to support them to enable them to win elections. Their difficulty is that key elements of the nativist agenda – restrictions on immigration, protectionism, nationalism, support for Brexit – tend to grate on other powerful and numerous components of the electorate, such as the highly educated, the young, those comfortable with internationalism and globalisation, making it difficult for national populist parties to gain ascendency over the incumbent parties.

The nativist vote is too important – even if it is a minority – for either of our major political parties to ignore, however. Rather than allowing nativist parties to erode their support, it therefore seems more likely that they will accommodate their stances and policies to try to garner potential populist votes without entirely abandoning their ideological moorings. In the current UK context, it is not difficult to portray current developments within the Conservative Party as electing a leader intent on swinging the Conservatives into a more populist electoral stance to attract C1 and C2 voters than they have now. This is not a long way from what has happened in the USA with the election of President Donald Trump. The result has been to pull the whole of the political spectrum considerably further to the right than it was before – reflecting the erosion of support for centre left parties described at the beginning of this book.

Conclusion

Developments along these lines do not look very encouraging for social democrats although, if the Conservative Party, in particular, makes a serious bid for national populist support, it may well strengthen the left-of-centre vote among the socially elite who, apart from anything else, control the media and thus much of opinion forming comment. The corresponding downside, however, for the centre left in the UK is that support is lost in Wales, the Midlands and the North where there are large numbers of traditional Labour voters in marginal seats who are likely to be attracted to a Conservative version of national populism. Of the 45 gains which Labour needs to make to have an overall majority in the House of Commons 35 have Leave majorities. From a gloomier Labour Party perspective, of the 20 most vulnerable seats if there is a swing away from Labour, 15 have Leave majorities.[28]

There is also the question of Labour's ideological position, which is nowadays substantially further to the left than it has been for many years. As has been very evident in the USA as well as the UK, this has attracted substantial highly committed support from quite a wide spectrum of the electorate in both age and socio-economic terms, but at the expense of putting off other more moderate-minded potential recruits to the cause. If this happens to a significant extent at the same time as Labour foregoes the support of a large section of its traditional support to whatever populist party emerges or to Conservatives with a distinctly more nativist agenda, the prospects for any left-of-centre government would be significantly reduced.

The challenge for both the existing main political parties is thus to attract enough of the nativist vote on the nativist/globalise spectrum without either losing core supporters or floating voters leaning in their direction on the more traditional left/right axis. The Brexit Party clearly has ambitions to develop from just fighting on EU issues to becoming more broadly based in policy terms, competing for both traditional Conservative and Labour votes.

In the longer term, however, it may well be that Labour will be more vulnerable because of its dependence on the alliance between working class and middle-class voters which may be more prone to fraying than the allegiances which keep the Conservative Party together. If this happens, we may well find that the Brexit Party becomes able to attract perhaps 15% or 20% of the electorate on a consistent basis, as UKIP used to do. Assuming that there is no change to our first-past-the-post electoral system, this may not be enough to elect a significant number of MPs to Parliament, but it may well take a sufficient amount of electoral support from Labour, especially if the current Lib Dem revival maintains momentum, to block the Labour Party from winning enough seats to be able to form a government If, on the other hand, both the Labour Party and the Conservatives continue to lose support, there may be an opportunity for a nationalist populist party such as the Brexit Party to break through, accompanied very probably by a substantial Lib Dem parliamentary contingent .

We face a very uncertain future.

5

Moving on from neoliberalism, where next for the centre-left?

The major lesson emerging from the analysis in this book is that the key failing of policies advocated and implemented by social democrats across the West, at least during the first two decades of the twenty-first century, has been on policies to achieve a reasonable rate of economic growth. It is this failure which has also dragged down the record of moderate left-of-centre governments on redistribution. In addition, it has to a significant extent been responsible for the cultural divides which have opened up. Growth has been too low to raise incomes and indeed, in far too many cases, to stop them falling. Globalisation has been allowed to hollow out manufacturing capacity across much of the West, as a result of inappropriate exchange rate policies. Investment has sagged, especially of the most productive varieties such as mechanisation, technology and power. Balance of payments deficits have plagued the UK and other countries, particularly the USA, which, as a result, have been unable by a wide margin to pay their way in the world, with the resulting deficits fuelling borrowing on a substantial and ultimately unsustainable scale. Increasing regional, intergenerational and socio-economic inequalities have been the consequence.

If economic growth had been greater and spread more evenly, it would have been possible for social democrats to have rolled back at least some of the increase in the post-tax and benefit Gini inequality which was Margaret Thatcher's UK legacy. If there had not been such a gap between the economic success of London and much of the rest of the country, there might well have been less of a gulf between the attitudes and life experiences of those living in the capital and those in the regions. But this is not what happened. The key issue is then whether any alternative economic policy might do much better.

The early chapters in this book point towards what social democrats need to do to regain the initiative. Whatever the merits of monetarism and neoliberalism in helping to curb the inflationary excesses of the 1970s and 1980s, they need to realise that fighting inflation is not nowadays the major problem. Despite very large increases in the monetary base – a rise, for example, of 1500% in the UK between 2000 and 2016[1] – there is little sign anywhere of price rises becoming a major problem, except in a few outlying countries with special circumstances such as Venezuela and Zimbabwe. Falling growth rates, however, have become the major issue for electorates throughout the western world.

Social democrats need, therefore, to change their primary economic policy goal from keeping inflation as close as possible to 2% to getting the economy to grow fast enough to raise living standards for almost everyone – and to rebalance the economy at the same time. The strategy for doing this must by now be familiar. We need to increase the proportion of GDP which we devote to investment from its current barely 16% in the UK to somewhere close to the world average of 25%.There needs to be a combination of increased public sector investment for social reasons but, critically, around half the increase needs to be devoted to the most productive categories of investment in terms of the contribution made to increasing gross value added. These are clustered around technology, mechanisation and power.

Nearly all this high-powered investment will, in the nature of things, take place in the private sector, primarily in light industry, where strong prospects of profitability are essential to drive investment, especially on the scale required. Unfortunately, this condition is nowhere near being fulfilled in the UK at the moment, as we can see from our record of deindustrialisation. This is because the UK cost base – all the costs incurred in sterling and charged out to the rest of the world through the prism of the exchange rate – is much too high for most light industry to be able to compete in world markets, as our record of deindustrialisation shows.

A parity for sterling of $1.30 or even $1.50 may work satisfactorily for UK service exports and for high-tech industries which do not operate in very price sensitive markets. It is, however, lethal for UK run-of-the-mill manufacturing which cannot compete against world competition with an exchange rate which is much too high in relation to our actual average levels of capital equipment and skill level per employee. If, to rebalance our economy, we need to get manufacturing as a percentage of GDP back up to something like 15%, we will never do so unless we have an exchange rate which makes it worth siting new light industrial plant and machinery in the UK, and not elsewhere, allowing for our current levels of productivity. The problem is that, to fulfil this condition, the UK needs an exchange rate which is much lower than we have at the moment, with sterling at around parity with the dollar. This is not where public opinion is at the moment, and this may well be social democracy's biggest challenge.

Look at what could be achieved however, if the required priority was given to getting the UK economy to be truly price competitive. The UK would still have the benefit of our strong export surplus in services, which runs at some £100bn a year. If it could then sell abroad the same proportion of our increased manufacturing output as is done with existing production, achieved by a combination of increased exports and import substitution, it would be possible to bring the UK's foreign payments position into rough balance, although it would probably be good policy for us to continue running a small deficit. Because all surpluses and deficits must balance out, getting rid of the UK's large foreign payment deficit is the only sure way of bringing government borrowing under control and ending the accumulation of more and more debt – through our government, as individuals, and as a nation.

As well as tackling the demand side of the UK's economy, there would then be much to be done on the considerably less controversial supply-side agenda. This would include key elements of the industrial strategy supply-side policies always favoured by the left – better education and training, less short-termism, expenditure on infrastructure and making finance rapidly available to manufacturing industry. It would also include significant policies favoured by the right – encouraging competition, using the tax system to favour business enterprise and market forces rather than detailed state intervention to provide the incentives needed. Pursuing a policy along these lines would also allow other key objectives to be achieved around redistribution inequality and empathy.

First, it would provide a way of dealing with the huge imbalances there are between London and the rest of the country. Reindustrialisation is by far the most realistic way of providing the areas of the UK outside London with the means of paying their way in the world, and thus stopping them being dependent on the current very large-scale subventions from the capital. If the North of England was more prosperous than the South, as it was until about 1920[2] – dependent as it then was on manufacturing – there is no reason why the current gap can't be closed. If it was done before, it can be done again.

Second, if this can be achieved, the very large calls on the tax and benefit system, which transfer resources from London to the regions to go some way to evening up post tax and benefit incomes compared to what they would otherwise have been, will no longer be necessary. This will free up anything up to £150bn in government funds – a huge sum representing about 7.5% of UK GDP – to be deployed for other purposes either for targeted expenditure, such as reducing austerity or alternatively to cut taxation.

Third, reindustrialisation would produce far better job prospects, particularly in the regions which are currently depressed, and which need them most, while also providing an opportunity for a big lift in the social as well as economic environment in areas which are badly in need of both. There would be a significant role for the state particularly in providing training and infrastructure improvements. Because London is so much more prosperous than the rest of the country, it currently receives the lion's share of governmental support, especially on infrastructure and education, because London's high level of economic activity makes these sorts of schemes look better value for money in the capital than elsewhere. This needs to change.

Fourth, by freeing up resources and improving job prospects, it should be possible to alleviate at least some of the inter-generational inequalities which are currently so apparent. Better opportunities, especially outside London should be one benefit. Another should be making finance available for a much larger house building programme than we have seen for many years. In the 1960s, the UK was building 300,000 units of accommodation a year. In the 2000s this total had fallen to less than 150,000, with the fall in social housing provision being even more marked.[3] No wonder millennials find it so difficult to establish themselves economically and to find a home of their own so that they can start a family.

Fifth, if we can spread prosperity across the whole country, reducing inter-regional transfers, it may be possible to do something to roll back the increase in inequality which became so much more marked during the 1980s when the post-tax and benefit Gini coefficient rose from 0.24 to 0.34. Nativists tend to be strong supporters of the welfare state, and providing stronger support for it has to be a key social democratic policy.

Finally, there is little doubt that the gulf in attitudes, aspirations and hope between London and the rest of the country has a large amount to do with the varying levels of optimism and confidence in the future which is responsible for such a large gap to be bridged between them. If we want to rebuild trust between London and the rest of the country – and between the electorate and our political elite – there is again no better way to start doing this than by evening up living standards across the country and providing well-financed public services to back them up. This is what social democrats need to be able to offer their electorates.

If industrial competitiveness in world markets is the key to the transition which needs to be accomplished and a lower exchange rate is needed to trigger the changes in incentives which have to be made to achieve this goal, we will never get there if the mantra is 2% inflation. It is this target that keeps the exchange rate too high, discourages investment, deindustrialises the country, causes our balance of payments deficits and borrowing, and generates inequality. If social democracy is to recover, social democrats need to be willing to take some more risks with inflation and to substitute growth targets for those based on corralling inflation at 2%.

Why is this not already happening? It is because there are genuine concerns about how viable a policy along these lines would be and these need careful consideration.

Countering objections to a more competitive pound

Many people, even if they were persuaded by the logic of the case for a more competitive exchange rate for sterling which has been presented in this book, might well be inclined to shy away from trying to implement it because of deeply held suspicions that such a policy would neither be achievable nor would it work even if it could be put into practice. What are these contentions and how can they be countered?

There are six main arguments which are regularly advanced to support these concerns. They are first that devaluation always produces extra inflation which negates any gains in competitiveness; second that devaluation is impossible to combine with an open economy; third that, if we did devalue, we would be bound to be met by retaliation which would undermine its benefit; fourth that reducing sterling's parity would make us all poorer; fifth that we have tried devaluation in the past and it does not work; and sixth that the UK is no good at manufacturing and that our economy would not therefore respond positively to a lower exchange rate. None of these allegations stands up to close scrutiny and a central part of the case put forward in this book is to understand why this is so.

Devaluation and inflation

The contention that devaluation always produces a rise in inflation is true in so far as it applies to goods and services which are imported. Price rises here are inevitable and a necessary part of switching demand from foreign to domestic suppliers. It does not, however, follow that the price level generally will rise more quickly than it would have done without a devaluation, and a wealth of evidence from the dozens of devaluations which have occurred among relatively rich and diversified economies such as ours in recent decades shows that in fact lower parities sometimes produce a little more inflation, sometimes a bit less, but most of the time little if any change from what would have happened anyway. This may seem a very surprising result to many people but this is unequivocally what the statistics show. Looking at recent examples, when the UK left the Exchange Rate Mechanism in 1992, sterling fell by a trade-weighted 12%,[4] while inflation fell from 5.9% in 1991 to 1.6% in 1993.[5] When sterling dropped from about $2.00 to the pound in 2007 to $1.50 in 2009, a drop of 25%, the rate of inflation barely flickered,[6] and what increase there was in 2011 was very largely driven by an increase in commodity prices affecting all countries, whose impact fell away as soon as they dropped back again.[7]

The reason why these are common outcomes is that, while higher import prices push up the price level, many factors to do with a lower parity tend to bring it down. Market interest rates tend to be lower after a devaluation, and so do tax rates. Production runs become longer, bringing down average costs. Investment, especially in the most productive parts of the economy, tends to rise significantly, increasing output per head, reducing costs and producing a wage climate more conducive to keeping income increases in line with productivity growth. Furthermore, as domestic supplies of goods and services become more competitive with those from abroad, demand switches to local sources, negating the need to pay higher import prices even if foreign suppliers reduce their prices to try to retain market share.

For all these reasons, the plain fact is that neither theory nor historical experience, based on a wide range of individual cases, show evidence of devaluations having any systematic effect on increasing inflation above what it would have been in any event. Still less does either theory or practice show that competitive gains from a devaluation tend rapidly to be eroded away by higher inflation, although this is a central tenet of monetarist thinking, which perhaps explains why so many people believe it to be the case even though this is not correct. On the contrary, the longer-term evidence very firmly indicates that economies which have strongly competitive international pricing tend to perform better and better as talent and highly productive investment is attracted to those sectors of the economy most likely to produce rising productivity and increasing competitiveness. This is the environment into which a considerably lower parity needs to draw the UK economy.

Changing the exchange rate in an open economy

Next, it is frequently contended that the parity of sterling is determined by market forces over which the authorities have little control, so that any policy to change the exchange rate in any direction is bound to fail. Again, historical experience indicates that this proposition cannot be correct. The Japanese, to provide a recent example, brought the parity of the yen down against the dollar by a third between the beginning of 2013 and the start of 2015[8] as a result of deliberate policy. Further back, the Plaza Accord, negotiated in 1985, produced a massive change in parities among the major trading nations of the world at the time, causing the dollar, for example, to fall against the yen by just over 50% between 1985 and 1987.[9]

It is of course true that market forces have a major influence on exchange rate parities but it does not follow from this that the authorities cannot influence the factors which determine what market outcomes are. If the UK pursues policies which makes it very easy for foreign interests to buy British assets, for example, this will exert a strong upward pressure on sterling's parity. If the Bank of England raises interest rates, this will also push sterling higher. If the Bank decides to keep the parity of the pound up, by buying sterling and selling dollars perhaps to bear down on inflationary pressures, this will have a correspondingly strengthening impact on sterling.

Sooner or later, the parlous state of our balance of payments is also likely to be a major factor. Up to now, the ability of the UK to finance its annual deficits by selling assets has tended to keep the markets confident that the rate at which sterling is trading on the foreign exchanges is sustainable. It is far from clear that this confidence will continue indefinitely for two main reasons. One is that the UK may soon have sold so many assets that it may become increasingly difficult to find enough to sell in future, especially if more safeguards relating to the sale of UK assets are put in place, thus making it more difficult to keep the exchange rate as high as it is at the moment. The second is that every £100bn annual deficit, financed by selling assets with an average gross return of the order of 2% to 3%, adds another £2bn to £3bn to the underlying deficit every year, as we forfeit the returns we would have had from the assets had we not sold them. It may, therefore, very well be the case that in the foreseeable future there will be a change in market sentiment – possibly associated with Brexit – which will bring sterling down to a lower parity with or without the assistance of the authorities. The fall in the value of sterling following the EU referendum in June 2016 has already shown this happening, although the fall from $1.45 to around $1.25 by summer 2019 is unfortunately still not enough to precipitate a large-scale industrial revival.

Retaliation

If the UK were to devalue by a sufficient amount – probably about 20% from its recent $1.25 level – to enable the economy to reindustrialise to a point where we could pay our way in the world – is it likely that there would be retaliation from other countries which would negate any benefits in the form of increased competitiveness which the devaluation had secured? The answer to this question needs to come in several parts.

In the first place, it depends on the position from which the devaluing country starts. The curse of foreign payment imbalances starts not with countries like the UK, with big deficits, but with countries such as Germany, Switzerland and the Netherlands with large surpluses – in 2017 about 8% of GDP in Germany's cases and 10% for the Netherlands' and Switzerland's.[10] These surpluses have to be matched by deficits somewhere else in the world economy. Unfortunately, surplus countries are never under any immediate pressure to reduce the beggar-thy-neighbour impact of their surpluses by revaluing their currencies and this leaves economies such as ours, carrying big deficits, with no alternative but devaluation to get the situation under control. There is thus a very strong principled case for countries such as the UK to make for getting sterling to a more competitive level.

In terms of practicalities, the UK has a number of advantages which other countries do not share. We are not in the EU's Single

Currency, membership of which would clearly preclude the UK from doing anything about our exchange rate. We still have our own central bank and control over our own interest rate and monetary policy. Sterling is not a world reserve currency like the dollar, making it much easier for us to alter our exchange rate without there being major international consequences. The fact that our share of world trade is now so low – at 2.5% in 2017[11] – means that what happens to sterling has relatively little impact on the rest of the world.

As to recent evidence, the quite major changes in the parity of sterling when the UK left the ERM in 1992 (a trade weighted drop of 12%)[12] and the fall in the rate for sterling against the dollar between 2007 and 2009 (about 25%)[13] as well as the post-EU referendum drop in sterling's parity, all engendered no retaliation. All were evidently seen by other countries – the markets and the authorities – as being exchange rate adjustments which were clearly warranted by the state of the UK economy. Against the background of our current high foreign exchange deficit, there is no reason why the same could not be made to happen again. If the manifest imbalances in the UK economy are clearly associated with an unsustainably high exchange rate this should also enable us to overcome any objections from our G7 partners, with whom we have jointly agreed not to indulge in unwarranted competitive devaluations.

Sterling and living standards

It is frequently argued that a devaluation must make us all poorer and this argument tends to take two forms, one of which is manifestly incorrect while the other can relatively easily be counteracted.

The first is that if we reduced the value of the pound by, say, 20%, in world currency terms, we would make ourselves 20% worse off and we would therefore genuinely be poorer by this amount. The fallacy with this argument is that, while it might be well-founded if we did all our shopping in international currencies such as dollars, this is not what UK residents do except perhaps when they go on holiday. UK citizens pay for almost everything they buy in sterling and it is therefore GDP measured in sterling, not in dollars, which counts. This is the way in which international accounting is done and this explains why IMF figures do not generally show falls in GDP when countries devalue. On the contrary, they almost invariably show the growth rate rising and GDP increasing in consequence. Since living standards closely approximate to GDP per head, especially over time, if the economy is increasing in size and the population does not change from what it would have been anyway, GDP per head and thus living standards must, as a matter of logic, go up rather than down.

The second potentially more substantial argument is that if we are going to increase our net trade balance to a point where we are not enjoying a standard of living far beyond what we are earning, as we are at the moment, living standards will have to suffer. Relatively speaking, this has to be correct. If we produce more for export, too, there will be less for the home market. Furthermore, if, to get the economy to grow faster, we have to spend a considerably higher proportion of our GDP than we do at the moment on investment, there will again have to be a corresponding reduction in consumption as a percentage of GDP. The crucial question then is whether the economy can be made to grow fast enough to enable both the shift towards exports and investment to be accommodated without living standards falling – indeed preferably rising. Careful calculations show that this would be possible – provided that a high enough proportion of increased investment goes to the most productive parts of the economy, mostly manufacturing. It can be done.[14]

Past devaluations

Sterling may be too strong now for the good of our manufacturing base, but there is a powerful case to be made that this is no new phenomenon. The outcome of controversies over banking prudence and the link between sterling and gold, combined with the dominance of financial interests over those of industry, all stretching back to the beginning of the nineteenth century when industrialisation in the UK really got under way, have always hobbled British industry. Although we initially showed the way on manufacturing, other countries have overtaken us as their industrial bases have got stronger and their more competitive currencies have allowed them to secure better net trade advantages.

As these other countries have invested more heavily in the future than we have, their output per head has grown more rapidly than ours, their wage climates have been better, and their inflation rates have been lower. As an extreme example, in Switzerland, between 1970 and 2010, the price level rose by 88%. In the UK it increased by 780%. The average annual Swiss inflation rate over these 40 years was 1.6% while in the UK it was 5.6%.[15] It was against this kind of background that from time to time the over-valuation of sterling became so obvious that either the markets or the authorities or both tolerated, engineered or encouraged the parity for sterling to fall. Perhaps it is worth reiterating the often-forgotten fact that sterling's fall by about 30% in 1931 – after near stagnation during the 1920s – enabled the UK economy to have its fastest peacetime spurt of growth ever during the middle of the 1930s: over 4% per annum cumulatively for the four years between 1933 and 1937.[16]

When World War II ended and the continent began to recover from wartime devastation, it soon became apparent that the UK had no chance of maintaining the pre-war dollar parity of $4.03 to the pound, and sterling was devalued in 1949 to $2.80.[17] Higher than average inflation in the UK than elsewhere and underinvestment in export industries resulted in a steady trade deterioration in the 1950s and 1960s, culminating in the pound being devalued in 1967 from $2.80 to $2.40.[18] Once currencies started to fluctuate against each other in the 1970s, following the break-up of the Bretton Woods fixed parity system in 1971,[19] rapidly rising prices combined with high interest rates kept sterling much too strong. This was especially so early in the 1980s and later in that decade as the UK entered the Exchange Rate Mechanism, which we left in 1992 to escape from a sharp economic downturn. After showing some signs of recovery, the UK economy then became more and more unbalanced as assets sales, starting in the late 1990s on a scale unparalleled anywhere else, pushed sterling up to extraordinarily high levels in the 2000s. Its value fell between 2007 and 2009 – still by not nearly enough – since when it has climbed back a bit and then fallen, post the EU referendum to roughly where we were in 2009. Meanwhile, in the East, over past decades, exactly the opposite policies were followed as they massively devalued.

The reality is that the UK's exchange rate has been muc.
strong to allow our industrial base to flourish for most of the
two centuries. The devaluations that have taken place have m
the situation rather better than it otherwise would have been, but
they have almost always been too little and too late.

Devaluation and the UK response

Finally, it is argued that the UK has no bent for manufacturing and
that, even if industry was presented with a much more favourable
competitive environment, it would not respond. While it is true that
a wide swathe particularly of low- and medium-tech manufacturing
is uneconomic in the UK at present, because the exchange rate
and the cost base derived from it are much too high, there is no
evidence whatever that, if more favourable conditions prevailed,
UK entrepreneurs would not be just as good as those anywhere
else in the world at taking advantage of the new opportunities
which would then open up.

Evidence for this proposition comes from a wide variety of
sources. Perhaps the most obvious is to consider how implausible
it is that the nation which was the very birthplace of the Industrial
Revolution should be incapable of running manufacturing
operations successfully, given a reasonably favourable environment.
Nor is there the slightest evidence that the UK lacks entrepreneurial
people who would be willing to try their hands at making money
out of making and selling, if the right opportunities were there.
The problem with the UK, as a manufacturing environment, is
that these conditions simply do not exist at the moment, because
the cost base is too high, and entrepreneurs rightly shun investing
in ventures which they can see from the beginning have poor
prospects of being profitable and successful.

The reason why the UK has allowed manufacturing as a
percentage of its GDP to fall from almost one third in 1970 to barely
10% now is obvious. Nearly all our internationally traded low- and
medium-tech manufacturing has been driven out of business and
there is insufficient high-tech activity – also subject to long term
threat – to fill the gap. We cannot allow this condition to continue if
our economy is to grow at a reasonable rate in future.

Transitioning to a new economic model

There is a well-trodden path by which advanced countries have allowed themselves to lose competitiveness, to deindustrialise, and to let their rate of economic growth slow up. This is the condition from which most of the West suffers, and there is really no example so far of this process being reversed. To undo this course in the UK is therefore going to involve covering new ground. What are the hurdles which need to be overcome to make sure that this happens?

The first problem is to persuade enough politicians, academics, civil servants and those who make up public opinion that there is a much better way ahead for our country than is at all likely to be achieved on present trends within the current neoliberal consensus. This is not going to be an easy task, not only because of the difficulties involved in getting any large number of people to change their minds, but also because most influential people are not particularly hard hit by the conditions in our economy which impact so adversely on many others. By and large, key opinion-formers enjoy high living standards and they and their families and friends are contented with their lot in life. The impact of low levels of investment, deindustrialisation, regional inequality, balance of payments deficits, and consumer and government borrowing on their personal lives is not very harsh and many rich people are more than content with the redistributive impact in their favour of neoliberal policies. The message from this book, however, is that nothing will materially change for the better until the realisation sinks in that the situation for a majority of the population is much worse than a lot of well-off people realise, as is all too clearly reflected in our current political discontents.

The second problem is the widely and firmly held view that devaluations always cause inflation and falling living standards because prices then rise faster than incomes. As explained above, however, history tells us otherwise. Table 5.1 shows what happened following all the major downward movements of the UK exchange rate which have taken place since 1931. In 1931 and 1992, prices subsequently actually fell substantially. After 1949 and 1967 there were rises but mainly because of other factors – rearmament for the Korean War in 1950 and a rash of inflationary strikes in 1968. Increases in price rises after 2008 and 2016 were modest. There is no evidence here of runaway inflation or of the extra price competitiveness achieved as a result of lower exchange rates being washed away by more rapid price increase than could reasonably have been expected anyway.

Year of devaluation	Overall devaluation (%)	Inflation previous year	Inflation devaluation year	Inflation devaluation year +1	Inflation devaluation year +2	Inflation devaluation year +3
1931	25%	−1.7%	−10.1%	−9.9%	−6.6%	+5.5%
1949	31%	5.1%	2.4%	2.7%	9.9%	6.3%
1967	16%	3.9%	2.7%	4.8%	5.4%	6.3%
1992	15%	5.9%	3.7%	1.6%	2.5%	3.4%
2008	22%	2.3%	3.6%	2.2%	3.3%	4.5%
2016	9%	0.1%	1.3%	2.6%	2.4%	1.9%

Table 5.1: Devaluation and Inflation

Sources: *One Hundred Years of Economic Statistics* by Thelma Liesner. London: Facts on File and the Economist, 1989, and successive editions of *International Statistics Yearbook. Washington DC, IMF.* Combined with data from the Office for National Statistics and https//inflationdata.com

Leaving aside the need to ensure that inflation stays within reasonable bounds, there are in fact only two other critical conditions which have to be met to ensure that the outcome will be the transformation in growth projections which a competitive exchange strategy is designed to achieve. One is that the responsiveness of exports and imports – the elasticity of demand for them – is sufficiently great to avoid the foreign payment balance getting out of hand. The other is that the social rate of return on investment – particularly if directed towards mechanisation, technology and power by the right price signals – will be of sufficient magnitude to generate the extra resources necessary to make the proposed policy work. Fortunately, there is ample evidence that both these key requirements can be met.

The evidence that the price sensitivity of UK exports and imports would be sufficiently high to get our foreign payments balance back under control if the exchange rate is sufficiently competitive comes both from world figures showing what the price sensitivity is generally for manufactured goods and from our own history. Recently the elasticity of demand for UK exports and imports does seem to have decreased substantially, but this is hardly surprising if nearly all our price sensitive manufacturing has been driven out of business. The key to this problem is to get the exchange rate down to a point where it is worth siting new manufacturing plant in the UK. This is what is needed to drive up the elasticities to where they need to be. Table 5.2 shows the results of a major research project undertaken by the IMF covering the early years of the twenty-first century clearly indicating that the UK is perfectly capable of meeting the Marshall-Lerner condition that the sum of elasticities must be more than unity for a devaluation to improve the trade balance.

Table 5.2: Elasticity of demand for exports and imports 2001-2004.			
	Export – long run	Import – long run	Total
Australia	0.70	1.61	2.31
Austria	1.20	0.88	2.08
Belgium	2.10	0.56	2.66
Canada	1.32	0.83	2.15
Czech Republic	0.82	1.20	2.02
Denmark	1.27	0.78	2.05
Finland	1.23	0.01	1.24
France	1.14	1.03	2.17
Germany	2.51	0.10	2.61
Greece	1.13	1.11	2.24
Hungary	0.88	0.83	1.71
Iceland	0.91	1.46	2.37
Ireland	0.84	0.34	1.18
Italy	0.99	0.97	1.96
Japan	1.72	0.75	2.47
Korea	1.02	0.21	1.23
Luxembourg	2.65	2.63	5.28
Netherlands	1.04	0.73	1.77
New Zealand	1.01	0.94	1.95
Norway	0.33	1.61	1.94

	Export – long run	Import – long run	Total
Portugal	1.65	1.46	3.11
Slovakia	0.84	0.83	1.67
Spain	1.08	1.33	2.41
Sweden	1.84	0.04	1.88
Switzerland	1.27	0.78	2.05
United States	1.77	1.52	3.29
United Kingdom	1.37	1.68	3.05
Mean	1.28	0.97	2.25
Median	1.14	0.88	2.02

Sources: Export Supply Elasticities Table 2, page 21, and Import Demand Elasticities Table 1, page 15 in *A Method for Calculating Export Supply and Import Demand Elasticities* by Stephen Tokarick. Washington DC: IMF Working Paper WP/10/180, published 2010. NB: signs have been reversed for imports in the table above for the sake of clarity.

As to the full, or social, rate of return which can be achieved on investment – especially on machinery, technology and power – Table 2.1 in Chapter 2 shows clearly what can be achieved in the right circumstances. Since most of this investment takes place in the privately-owned tradable sectors of the economy, the key requirement to make it happen is the profitability, which a competitive exchange rate will deliver. In essence, as set out previously, the way to get the UK economy to grow at about 3.5% per annum instead of 1.5% is to shift 4% of UK GDP out of consumption and into high powered investment which has a social rate of return of at least 50% a year. This will increase the growth rate by 4% x 50%, which is 2% per annum.

This is the strategy which will deliver sustainable growth for the UK economy at about the world's average rate. If social democracy is to become a dominant force in the land again, this is the economic narrative which it needs to embrace.

Conclusion

It's the economy, stupid

The UK is currently in turmoil over Brexit. Dealing with the outcome of the 2016 referendum has dominated the political agenda for more than three years and it is still far from clear what the eventual outcome will be. What bearing does this disarray have on the near- and long-term prospects for social democracy, especially in the UK?

For the first few months of 2019, both Labour and the Conservatives were doing reasonably well in the polls. After the UK's failure to leave the EU at the end of March 2019, however, both parties haemorrhaged support, producing disastrously poor results for both of them in the May 2019 European elections, although the Conservatives did manage by early autumn to re-establish what may turn out to be a fragile recovery. Electoral volatility on this scale makes any forward projections or predictions especially speculative and insecure. The only near certainty is that social democracy in the form of a Labour government elected on a moderate platform is not on the agenda if – as seems very likely – a general election is held either late in 2019 or early in 2020.

It may be that Labour's fortunes will pick up over the coming year or two, if only as a result of the Conservative Party being in disarray. Labour might then be able to win an early general election because of right-of-centre votes being split between the Conservatives and the Brexit Party, while support for other parties falls back. If this happens, a relatively far-left Labour Party will then have a chance to test its credibility with the electorate. Buttressed by our first-past-the-post system, it may be able to hold at bay competition from the Liberal Democrats, the Greens, the SNP and Plaid Cymru.

The chances of events turning out in this way do not, however, look high. It may be that traditional allegiances, which recent polls show to be so heavily fractured, especially if the terms on which the UK is to leave the EU remain unresolved, will revert back towards those held before the European elections, when both Labour and Conservatives were on 25%, the Brexit Party on 18% and the Lib Dems on 16%.[1] The extent to which this might happen may, however, be limited. Of those Labour Party members who voted, 41% did so for other parties. Furthermore, a large-scale poll undertaken by Lord Ashcroft just after the elections showed that about half of all former Labour and Conservative voters who switched to other parties during the European elections did not intend to revert to their previous allegiances.[2] If the Conservatives do relatively but not disastrously poorly, a coalition government may then be the outcome with Labour trying to find a common platform – or at least a working arrangement – with some combination of the Lib Dems, the SNP and other minor parties.

The short-term problem for Labour is that the compromise policy which it has pursued on Brexit – essentially trying to appeal to Leavers by claiming that it was committed to Brexit while becoming more and more Remain-oriented because of membership pressure – has failed to work. Calls for a second referendum have been generally seen as no more than the way to provide the Labour Party with democratic cover for reversing the 2016 EU referendum result – albeit if the result of a second referendum turns out to be the Remain outcome they want, which is far from certain. This half-hearted commitment to Remain has further alienated Leave-oriented Labour supporters, while allowing Labour to be outflanked by the Lib Dems and other parties openly campaigning for revocation of Article 50 and the UK staying in the EU. Hence Labour's poor poll ratings.

Opinions among the electorate have become increasingly polarised. Many Remain voters among the electorate want to elect a government with a clear mandate to keep the UK in the EU, while many Leavers would be prepared to leave the EU on 'No Deal' World Trade Organization (WTO) trading terms, if no better deal than this can be negotiated. The most likely way ahead, nevertheless, seems to be that the Labour Party will flinch from campaigning at least in the immediate future for outright withdrawal, while continuing to advocate a second referendum at which it would campaign for Remain, even though this relatively half-hearted approach to keeping the UK in the EU appears to have decreasing electoral support. This stance therefore seems unlikely to lead to Labour recovering in the polls.

The analysis in this book, however, suggests that the party's handling of Brexit may be a symptom of a much deeper and more critical malaise, which may make recovery in Labour's fortunes more difficult to achieve. Labour's problem, reflected in the experience of social democrats right across the West, is not just that it has been torn apart by Brexit. This is hardly surprising and has been very difficult to avoid when 90% of its MPs and probably 80% of its membership are staunchly in favour of Remain while anything up to half of its traditional electorate are in the Leave camp. It is that Labour's failure to find a way to handle its Brexit dilemmas reflects the fundamental problem for all those in different countries involved in trying to hold together the moderate left alliance between its middle-class adherents – mostly globalisers – and its working-class supporters, who are largely nativists. The danger is that there simply is not enough common interest, respect and fellow-feeling between them in the UK – as in other countries – to maintain the cohesion needed to re-achieve electoral success for moderate left-of-centre parties.

What, if anything, can be done to reverse this trajectory and to bring the Labour Party in the UK back towards a social democratic rather than a democratic socialist stance with a reasonable prospect of winning elections? There are clearly strong forces pushing Labour, with its current policies, towards becoming only one of several non-Conservative parties competing with very roughly equal weight for votes with the Lib Dems and the SNP in Scotland and Plaid Cymru in Wales. If this happens, Labour may continue with its current relatively far-left policies – pursuing broadly the type of democratic socialist agenda favoured by Jeremy Corbyn and Jean-Luc Mélenchon in France and Bernie Sanders in the USA – as distinct from social democracy. There is no doubt that policies along these lines appeal to a significant section of the electorate across the West, but not much sign that they are likely to attain anything like the government-forming breadth of support which social democrats used to be able to achieve.

What will then happen to social democracy? It seems unlikely that the large-scale latent support for moderate left-of-centre policies will be unable to find expression somehow in the political system in the UK and elsewhere. The issue is whether it is likely to take the form of relatively small and ineffectual parties advocating broadly the same agenda as has failed social democracy during the first two decades of the twenty-first century. Alternatively, can the existing left-of-centre parties – especially Labour in the UK – pivot back to a more social democratic rather than democratic socialist stance and, with new and updated policies, recapture enough electoral support to become again in future a serious contender for government power.

In the UK context, a lot will depend on what happens to the Conservative and Brexit parties and the general realignment of political allegiances along the nativist/globalist, rather than left/right axis, which appears to be taking place. It seems likely that the nationalist populist policies advocated by the Brexit Party are going to have a continuing presence on the political scene, but probably not on the scale they have recently had once – one way or another – the present salience of Brexit drops away. If the Brexit Party – possibly renamed – settles down with a broadly nativist agenda appealing to 15% to 20% of the electorate, this may deprive the Conservative Party of any likelihood of gaining an outright majority. It may also, however, also entail loss of support for Labour among their traditional supporters as a significant proportion of them move their support to the Brexit Party. The issue then is whether social democrats can forge a policy agenda of enough attractiveness and weight to continue to be a major political force by holding together sufficient of the alliance of middle- and working-class support that does not defect to the Brexit Party's nativist agenda.

The message in this book is that a revival of social democracy may be possible, but for this to happen there will have to be major shifts in perception and policy which may be difficult but not impossible to achieve. On the economic front, as long as the neoliberal framework for policy formation remains in place and containing inflation at 2% remains the top economic priority, the exchange rate will be too high, investment will be much too low, our manufacturing industries will flag, we will continue to fail to pay our way in the world, our borrowings will increase and inequality will not be reversed and may get more acute. This is not a policy environment in which social democracy is likely to be able to offer a sufficiently enticing vision for the future to win elections.

On top of all the other difficulties there are about making redistribution work effectively, as long as there are such huge disparities as there are at present between London and the regions, much of our tax and benefit system will continue to be pre-empted to offsetting the massive differences in earning power between London and the rest of the country – for which deindustrialisation is mainly responsible. There will then continue to be little scope for arresting or reversing the very large increase in inequality which took place in the 1980s. The issue then is whether, by radical changes to our economic policies, globalisation can be made to enhance incomes and life chances for enough of the population to offset the appeal of nativist policies. Then there may be a social democratic policy agenda robust and appealing enough to win elections.

It was James Carville, a campaign strategist in Bill Clinton's successful 1992 presidential campaign against president George HW Bush, who coined the phrase 'It's the economy, stupid'. The analysis presented here suggests that he was right not only for the USA nearly 30 years ago but for the UK – and indeed for the whole of the West – now. If we want our politics to move forward on the rational and caring basis for which social democracy stands, we will never do so unless we can get our economy to perform better, to provide hope and succour not just to a lucky few but to everyone.

Notes

Introduction

1 Lord Ashcroft poll distributed March 2019. Bagehot in *The Economist,*
6th April 2019.

Chapter 1

1 Chapter 3 in Economic and Fiscal Outlook – March 2019. London: Office for
Budget Responsibility, 2019.
2 ONS population statistics; London: ONS, 2019.
3 Monthly Wages and Salaries Survey. London: ONS, 2018.
4 Government estimate of the cost of climate change to 2050. Summer 2019.
5 Page 75 in *International Monetary Statistics Yearbook 2018.* Washington DC:
IMF, 2018.
6 Wikipedia entry on Bretton Woods.
7 Page 164 in *International Monetary Financial Statistics.* Washington DC: IMF, 1989.
8 Ibid, page 184.
9 Pages 186 and 187 in *International Financial Statistics Yearbook 1989.*
Washington DC: IMF, 1989.
10 Page 124 in *International Monetary Financial Statistics.* Washington DC: IMF,
2000.
11 Investopedia.com entry on the Stability and Growth Pact.
12 Successive issues of *International Financial Statistics Yearbook.* Washington DC:
IMF.
13 Pages 174 to 177 in *Main Economic Indicators.* Paris: OECD, 1999.
14 Table 20, pages 128 and 129 in *National Accounts 1960-1992.* Paris: OECD,
1994.
15 Wikipedia entry on the 1923 German hyperinflation.
16 Wikipedia entry on *List of Countries* by Steel Production.
17 Wikipedia entry on *List of Countries* by Motor Vehicle Production.
18 Wikipedia entry on *A Monetary History of the United States.*
19 Table 5.2, page 228 in *Economic Trends 1996/97 Annual Supplement.* London:
Office for National Statistics, 1997.
20 Pages 88 and 89 in *International Financial Statistics.* Washington DC: IMF, 1998.
21 Table B-69 in *Economic Report of the President.* Washington DC. US
Government Printing Office, 2011.
22 Ibid, Table B-1.

Chapter 2

1 ONS code NPQT as a percentage of YBHA. London: ONS March 2019.
2 Page 829 in *International Statistics Yearbook 2017*. Washington DC: IMF, 2017.
3 Ibid, page 86.
4 ONS code NPQT as a percentage of YBHA. London: ONS, March 2019.
5 ONS codes NPQT minus EQDO divided by YBHA. London: ONS, March 2019.
6 Consumption of fixed capital in the UK in 2016 was 12.9% of GDP. Page 829 in *International Financial Statistics Yearbook. Washington DC: IMF*, 2017.
7 ONS code DLWO divided by YBHA. London: ONS, March 2019.
8 ourworldindata,org website.
9 Wikipedia entry on Agriculture in the UK.
10 Table J.1 in *Economic Statistics 1900-1983* by Thelma Liesner. London: The Economist 1985.
11 Table C-16a, page 183, in *Monitoring the World Economy* by Angus Maddison. Paris: OECD, 1995.
12 Ibid, Table US.1.
13 Ibid, Table UK.1.
14 Calculated from tables in *International Statistics Yearbook 2017*. Washington DC: IMF 2017.
15 Ibid.
16 Ibid.
17 Ibid, including some ONS data.
18 Bank of England website.
19 Page 980 in *International Statistics Yearbook 2000*. Washington DC: IMF 2000.
20 Table 7.1, page 66, in the 2011 Pink Book. London: ONS, 2011.
21 Page 745 in *International Statistics Yearbook 2010*. Washington DC: IMF 2000.
22 Page 7 in *Economic Review March 2014*. London: ONS, 2014.
23 www.economicshelp.org/blog/7617/economics.
24 Calculations based on ONS codes ABMI and YBEX. London: ONS, December 2017.
25 Table 4.1 covering Trade Flows for London, the rest of the UK, and the UK from production and total output, £bn 2013. The London input-output tables, working paper 97.
26 ONS Regional GVA Income Approach. ONS. London: ONS, 2016.
27 Data from Trading Economics website. At the end of 2017 wages in manufacturing averaged £595 per week compared to an overall average of £510.
28 ONS code BOK!. London: ONS, 2018.
29 ONS codes ELBH plus ELBI. London: ONS, 2018.
30 ONS code HBOP divided by YBHA. London: ONS, 2018.
31 ONS code L877. London: ONS, 2018.
32 ONS code L871. London: ONS, 2018.
33 Tables in successive editions of *International Monetary Statistics Yearbook*. Washington DC: IMF.

34 Ibid.
35 The total was £1.057trn. ONS code BOKI. London: ONS, 2018.
36 Page 80 in International Monetary Statistics 2017. Washington DC: IMF, 2017
37 Bank of England website.
38 Page 88 in *International Statistics Yearbook 2017*. Washington DC: IMF, 2017.
39 Data extracted from *North and South* by David Smith. London: Penguin Books, 1989.
40 Wikipedia entry on Bradford.
41 Calculated from ONS NUTS2 data.
42 Table 224 in House building permanent dwellings completed by tenure historical calendar year series. London: ONS, 2015.
43 Ibid.
44 Figures taken from an article by Liam Halligan in the Sunday Telegraph June 2019.
45 BETA house Price Index.
46 FTSE 100 Historical Data.
47 Distribution of total wealth for Great Britain and London (July 2010- June 2014). London: ONS, 2015.

Chapter 3

1   Wikipedia entry on the Independent Labour Party.
2   House of Commons History of the Parliamentary Franchise. London: March 2013.
3   Wikipedia entry on the Labour Party.
4   Wikipedia entry on Clause 4.
5   Wikipedia entry on Public Ownership.
6   Wikipedia entry on the History of Taxation in the United Kingdom.
7   Table B-10A, page 151 in *Monitoring the World Economy 1820-1992* by Angus Maddison. Paris: OECD, 1995.
8   Wikipedia entry on the Labour Party.
9   www.ukpblicspending.co.uk.
10 Wikipedia entry on The Post-War Consensus.
11 Table C1-b, Page 273, in *Monitoring the World Economy 1820-1992* by Angus Maddison. Paris: OECD, 1995.
12 Page 147 in *Capital in the Twenty-First Century* by Thomas Piketty. Cambridge, Mass: Harvard University Press, 2014.
13 Ibid, pages 316 and 317.
14 Ibid page 316.
15 Pew Centre report dated 7th August 2018.
16 Low Pay Britain report by the Resolution Foundation, 2018.
17 Wikipedia entry covering the UK Gini Coefficient.
18 Page 75 in International *Monetary Statistics Yearbook 2010*. Washington DC: IMF 2010.

19 Reports on the Kraft takeover of Cadbury's indicated that total City fees came to 3% of the price Kraft paid. Using this ratio for all the assets sales to foreign interests arranged by the City between 2000 and 2010 produces total charges of about £40bn.
20 Page 75 in *International Monetary Statistics Yearbook 2018*. Washington DC: IMF, 2018.
21 *Das Kapital* by Karl Marx. Successive editions.
22 Wikipedia entry on The Future of Socialism.
23 Table C-16a in *Monitoring the World Economy 1820-1992* by Angus Maddison. Paris: OECD, 1995.
24 Ibid, Table c-16c.
25 Nikita Krushchev (1894-1971) made a speech in 1959 at the United Nations claiming that Soviet living standards would soon outstrip those in the USA.
26 Wikipedia entry on Leonid Brezhnev.
27 www.hisory.com entry on The Berlin Wall.
28 Wikipedia entry on public ownership.
29 Wikipedia entry on State Owned Enterprises of the United Kingdom.
30 Wikipedia entry on Adam Smith.
31 *Adam Smith: What He Thought and Why It Matters* by Jesse Norman. London: Penguin 2018.
32 YouGov report dated May 2017 on renationalising the UK railway system.
33 ONS Regional GVA Income Approach. London: ONS, 2016.
34 www.theactuary.com.
35 www.housing.org.uk website.
36 Report in *The Guardian* 20th April 2015.
37 GDP at Regional Level. Brussels: Eurostat, 2018.
38 ONS Regional GVA Income Approach. London: ONS, 2016.
39 ONS Labour Force #survey: London: ONS, 2019.
40 Report in *The Guardian* 1st June 2017.
41 BBC news report 10th May 2019.
42 Wikipedia entry on the Barnett Formula.
43 YouGov poll 2017.

Chapter 4

1   Data from Lord Ashcroft polling.
2   Data from Education: Historical statistics, 27th November 2012, House of Commons Library.
3   Wikipedia entry on Clement Attlee's cabinets.
4   Social Background of Members of Parliament. House of Commons Library. London, 2017.
5   www.ourworlindata,org website.
6   ONS Table LPROD02.
7   Calculations based on ONS codes ABMI and YBEX.
8   Calculated from ONS NUTS2 data.
9   Data from Trading Economics website At the end of 2017 wages in

manufacturing averaged £595 per week compared to an overall average of £510.

10 www.uscensus.gov.data
11 Wikipedia entry on Enlargement of the European Union.
12 ONS population statistics.
13 Information provided by Google.
14 Social Mobility Commission, *State of the Nation* 2017.
15 Europa.eu website.
16 Ibid.
17 Wikipedia entry on the Eurozone.
18 Successive editions of *International Financial Statistics*. Washington DC: IMF.
19 Ibid.
20 Wikipedia entry on Ethnic Groups in London.
21 Answer to Google question.
22 Medical Women's Federation website.
23 Full Fact website.
24 Lord Ashcroft polling.
25 YouGov poll, 2017.
26 Wikipedia entry on European political parties.
27 BBC report on the 2017 general election and Wikipedia entry on previous elections.
28 Wikipedia analysis of the 2017 general election results.

Chapter 5

1 ONS and IMF publications.
2 Data from *North and South* by David Smith. London, Penguin Books, 1985.
3 ONS Table 224 House building permanent dwellings completed by tenure historical calendar years series.
4 Page 981 in *International Financial Statistics Yearbook 2000*. Washington DC: IMF, 2000.
5 Ibid, page 125.
6 Page 66 in *International Financial Statistics Yearbook 2014*. Washington DC: IMF, 2014.
7 Ibid, pages 89 to 91.
8 www.xe.com website.
9 Wikipedia entry on the Plaza Accord.
10 Country tables in *International Financial Statistics Yearbook 2018*. Washington DC: IMF, 2018.
11 Ibid, Exports FOB Table, page 69.
12 Page 981 in *International Financial Statics Yearbook 2000*. Washington DC: IMF, 2000
13 www.xe.com website.
14 The necessary calculations are contained in John Mills and Bryan Gould, *Call to Action: Britain's economic problems and how they can be solved* (London: Ebury Publishing, 2015).

15 Producer Prices/Wholesale Prices 1970 to 1999, pages 120 and 121 in
    *International Financial Statistics Yearbook 2000; Prices: Home and Imported Goods
    for Switzerland, 1999 to 2010, page 696 and prices for manufacturing output for the
    UK, page 742* in international Financial Statistics Yearbook 201. Washington
    DC: IMF, 2012.
16 Table UK1 in *Economic Statistics 1900-1983* by Thelma Liesner. London: The
    Economist, 1985.
17 Ibid, Table UK.15.
18 Ibid.
19 Wikipedia entry on Bretton Woods.

Conclusion

1   YouGov poll report.
2   Lord Ashcroft polling report.